# The Decision
# for American
# Independence

J. R. Pole
Churchill College
Cambridge University

**The America's Alternatives Series**

Edited by **Harold M. Hyman**

# The Decision for American Independence

**J. B. Lippincott Company**
Philadelphia/New York/Toronto

ISBN 0-397-47330-3
Library of Congress Catalog Card Number 74-23097
Printed in the United States of America

1 3 5 7 9 8 6 4 2

Library of Congress Cataloging in Publication Data

Pole, Jack Richon.
    The decision for American independence.

    (The America's alternatives series)
    Bibliography: p.
    1.  United States—Politics and government—Revolution, 1775-1783.
I.   Title.
E210.P63            973.3'1            74-23097
ISBN 0-397-47330-3

For Ilsa Pole

# Contents ═══════════════

# Foreword

"When you judge decisions, you have to judge them in the light of what there was available to do it," noted Secretary of State George C. Marshall to the Senate Committees on the Armed Services and Foreign Relations in May 1951.[1] In this spirit, each volume in the "America's Alternatives" series examines the past for insights which History—perhaps only History—is peculiarly fitted to offer. In each volume the author seeks to learn why decision makers in crucial public policy or, more rarely, private choice situations adopted a course and rejected others. Within this context of choices, the author may ask what influence then-existing expert opinion, administrative structures, and budgetary factors exerted in shaping decisions? What weights did constitutions or traditions have? What did men hope for or fear? On what information did they base their decisions? Once a decision was made, how was the decision maker able to enforce it? What attitudes prevailed toward nationality, race, region, religion, or sex, and how did these attitudes modify results?

We freely ask such questions of the events of our time. This "America's Alternatives" volume transfers appropriate versions of such queries to the past.

In examining those elements that were a part of a crucial historical decision, the author has refrained from making judgments based upon attitudes, information, or values that were not current at the time the decision was made. Instead, as much as possible he or she has explored the past in terms of data and prejudices known to persons contemporary to the event.

---

[1] U.S., Congress, Senate, Hearings Before the Committees on the Armed Services and the Foreign Relations of the United States, *The Military Situation in the Far East*, 82d cong., 2d sess., part I, p. 382. Professor Ernest R. May's "Alternatives" volume directed me to this source and quotation.

Nevertheless, the following reconstruction of one of America's major alternative choices speaks implicitly and frequently, explicitly to present concerns.

In form, this volume consists of a narrative and analytical historical essay (Part One), within which the author has identified the choices which he believes were actually before the decision makers with whom he is concerned.

Part Two of this volume contains, in whole or part, the most appropriate source documents that illustrate Part One. In turn, Part One will direct readers to appropriate Part Two Documents. The volume's Part Three offers users further guidance in the form of a Bibliographic and Historiographical Essay.

When the Continental Congress voted for American independence in 1776, it seemed a dangerous and fateful step. Yet soon afterward, Americans began to think of it as inevitable, and that attitude has grown stronger during the two hundred years of the nation's existence. Folklore has encrusted the attitude, and reverance has contributed to it. Moreover, something of a gap has developed between historical scholars and the general public in the ways they have come to understand the events of that period. The approach of the bicentennial of the American Revolution gives us a welcome and perhaps a necessary opportunity to try to close that gap by bringing the best results of historical learning to bear on the general interpretation of the decision for American independence.

Dr. J. R. Pole of Cambridge University is a British scholar who, during the last twenty years, has contributed to the study of American history from the seventeenth century to the twentieth. In this volume he retraces the course taken by America's nation-builders in the years 1775-1776, and shows how they thought about the choices that lay before them and how they decided among those choices. In the national sense, this was the first set of America's Alternatives.

Harold M. Hyman
Rice University

# Acknowledgment

In preparing and checking the material for this book I have received inestimable help from Dr. J. R. Zvesper of Peterhouse, Cambridge.

# Part One

## The Decision

# 1

## The First Continental Congress

### Inspirations for a Colonial Congress

American independence had many prophets. Taking a long view of the growth of the colonies, it was not difficult to foresee the general prospect that they would one day be too big to be governed by the mother country. When Peter Kalm, a Swedish botanist, travelled in the middle and northern colonies during the mid-1740s, he found people talking freely of the possibility that the Americans would be independent of Great Britain within thirty to fifty years.[1] Some years afterwards, Benjamin Franklin published his famous essay, *Observations Concerning the Increase of Mankind* (1751), in which he estimated that the population of the colonies was doubling every twenty-five years, which meant that, within another century "the greatest Number of Englishmen will be on this Side of the Water." He saw this vast increase as a great accession of power to the British Empire. As all these people were British subjects, this could mean that the seat of the empire would be transferred to America. To others, of course, it could mean ultimate separation. From the standpoint of later history, it is easy—perhaps deceptively easy—to recognize that American independence was ultimately inevitable.

To classify an event as inevitable, however, is to deprive it of historical significance, since it divests the people involved in the event of all power of making their own decisions. There are certainly moments in history at which we can say that an event had become inevitable; but that means that the historical problem has to be reformulated and a new question asked: when, and for what reasons, did the event under consideration become inevitable? It cannot always have been inevitable. If that were so, there would be no history to write, only a record of involuntary acts of submission. The historian must concern himself with the problem of how a situation changed, constantly redefining and altering the choices available to the people who had to decide. Equally important is the question of the precise timing of the event. It is reasonably safe, for example, to say that American independence was inevitable at some period between 1760 and 1850; but it makes a vast difference not only to Americans but to much of the rest of the world that it took place earlier rather than later in that span of time. American independence in the period 1776-1783 was—and remains—a different event from an imagined American secession from Britain in 1850, or at any other time.

The men who arrived in Philadelphia during the last days of August and the early days of September, 1774, did not regard American independence as inevitable. They had come, for the first time in American history, to form a general congress of the colonies, with the object of working out and concerting colonial action against the British government. Only a small minority among them had already made up their minds that the right solution was to renounce their allegiance to the king and to dissolve their connection with the British nation. The Massachusetts cousins, Samuel and John Adams, had been thinking on these lines for several years—perhaps as far back as 1768, when British troops moved into Boston to keep order there. Patrick Henry of Virginia, who had moved certain fiery resolutions denouncing the Stamp Act in the Virginia House of Burgesses, was probably also ready to take the extreme step, and he had a close sympathizer in his colleague, Richard Henry Lee. Christopher Godsden of South Carolina was equally impatient; others could be found. But these men came to Philadelphia knowing that their views were widely regarded with abhorrence. They did not have to spend long in the process of getting to know members of other delegations before they discovered that the opposition to thoughts of independence was fully as deep as they had feared, that it was widespread, and that it reflected the outlook of men who wielded great influence both in their own provinces and in the Congress.

The original inspiration of the Continental Congress was in fact as much conservative as it was radical. The call came out of an exchange of letters between Boston and New York, in May, 1774, as well as from initiatives in other colonies at about the same time. When the news of the Boston Port Act, which closed the port until the tea destroyed in the Tea Party had been paid for, arrived in the city on May 10, the Boston Committee of Correspondence at once convened to consider retaliatory action. Samuel Adams, who dominated these proceedings, persuaded the committee to propose a Solemn League and Covenant—the language deliberately recalled the agreement of the English and the Scots in 1644—with the object of renouncing British imports. This plan was extremely unpopular with the merchants of Boston itself, and soon foundered when messengers carried it south to other provinces.

Merchants throughout the colonies saw little merit in these puritanical proposals for self-abnegation, which inflicted much more immediate hardship on the people of the colonies than on the British. The last set of nonimportation agreements had proved excessively difficult to maintain and did not achieve notable success. New York City had a committee to work out local policies in the struggle with British authority, and the composition and attitudes of this committee reflected the complicated maneuvering for power within New York itself. The traditionally influential and socially conservative merchants and greater landowners had very good reasons for alarm at the way in which the mechanics, or artisans, allied with small traders and people of lesser substance, were using the quarrel with Britain as a powerful means of leverage, particularly in the politics of the city. The conservatives entered into the popular committees that were created to concert resistance to British policies, but they did so as much to control them, and keep their measures within bounds that would be safe from the point of view of the internal struggle for power, as for the larger purpose of protecting American liberties. One of the most influential of the New York conservatives, Robert R. Livingston, looking back on this phase, explained the attitude when he commented on a similar situation faced by kindred interests in Pennsylvania: "I long ago advised that they should yield to the torrent if they hoped to avert its course—you know nothing but well timed delays, indefatigable industry, and a minute attention to every favourable circumstance, could have prevented our being in exactly the same situation."[2] Gouverneur Morris, an aggressively conservative New York aristocrat, graphically illustrated the social character of the struggle in his description of a mass meeting held in the spring of 1774: "I stood in the balcony and on my right hand were ranged all the people of property with some few poor dependents, and on the other all the tradesmen." Thus arrayed against each other, they "fairly contended about the future form of our government, whether it should be founded on Aristocratic or Democratic principles."[3]

## Conservative Fears and Interests

Two kinds of conservatism can be found among the different delegations, though they do not exclude each other. The first was by far the most influential. It arose from the fear that independence, which could be achieved only by war, would lead to social upheaval, overthrowing the old families from their seats of political power, and threatening the advantages enjoyed by powerful economic interests. Merchants who held a grip on seaborne commerce and on the domestic marketing of goods owed at least some of their power to the protection of existing legislation; the great landlords along the Hudson River had already been disturbed by rent riots. The confusing but intoxicating upsurge of rebellion might easily spill over into their own domains. Men with these interests to defend in New York, and men of like minds and interests in such centers as Philadelphia, Annapolis and Charleston, as well as landlords with disaffected tenants in rural areas of Maryland and the Carolinas, had reason to fear that the social insurgents in their midst would get a grip on the enforcement of a new wave of nonimportation agreements, and had little taste for such measures. Any thought of independence was very remote from their minds, except as an evil to be avoided.

To identify these groups as being concerned with the maintenance of stability in their own cities and provinces is not to deny their legitimate concern for the defense of American liberties. In the terminology which would soon acquire specific connotations for American patriotism, they were Whigs. They held firmly to principles of representative government under colonial charters and the British constitution, and no radical could have believed more firmly that a freeborn Englishman could never be separated from his money by taxation without his own consent. They believed implicitly in the English common law, with its cardinal doctrines of the inviolability of a person's home and the right of trial by juries drawn from the immediate locality. It was quite as clear to them as to their own dissidents that the Massachusetts Government Act, by which Parliament revoked vital clauses of the colony's charter, made the council appointive, and closed down the famous town meetings except with the governor's permission, subverted the constitutional liberties of the Bay Colony, and held a more distant but distinct threat to the liberties of others.

Nevertheless, as the Massachusetts radicals soon found, these more conservative delegates regarded Bostonians with some suspicion. The city had earned a widespread reputation for violence and disorder, coupled with socially leveling tendencies that did not endear them to the dignified representatives whose very presence in Philadelphia reflected the selective principles of a highly deferential social order. The celebrated Tea Party itself had been a spectacular affront to private property. Whatever their feelings about the legal complexities may have been, merchants and men of property entertained understandable doubts about the social consequences when the leaders of Boston society gave their approval to gangs of unopposed but heavily disguised citizens who took it upon themselves to deposit several thousands of pounds worth of other peoples' property into the sea. In Philadelphia, the delegates to Congress had plenty of opportunities of meeting the socially prominent merchant classes, many of them Quakers. They had been deeply suspicious of Boston since the last nonimportation agreement in 1769, which had aroused sharp mutual recriminations. The situation in Pennsylvania was greatly complicated by the history of a bitter struggle between the old assembly majority, led for many years by Joseph Galloway and his ally Benjamin Franklin, and on the other side the proprietors of the province. The Proprietary party had managed to enlist the Scotch-Irish Presbyterians of the newly settled west. Franklin and Galloway had been engaged for several years in trying to unseat their enemies by persuading the crown to take back the charter—it was for this purpose that Franklin had spent several years in England. John Dickinson had long been identified politically as an opponent of Franklin and Galloway, a position he had no desire to drop when he emerged as the author of the *Letters of a Pennsylvania Farmer*.[4] With the old leadership locked in this relentless feud, a new, highly radical group embodying the economic grievances and social ambitions of the Philadelphia mechanics and small traders, broke very rapidly into the political arena while the Continental Congress was meeting in the city. Franklin himself remained for the time being in England; it was he who presented the declarations of the Congress to Lord Dartmouth, secretary of state for the American colonies. But he returned to join the Second Continental Congress in May, 1775, and just in time to establish his reputation as an American patriot rather than a wary opportunist.

These internal divisions affected the attitude of Pennsylvania down to the last two months before the Declaration of Independence. In a similar fashion, the influential New York conservatives actually held back the assembly's agreement until after the Declaration had been agreed upon by the Congress. Another colony afflicted with this brand of conservatism was Maryland, where the great families of the eastern shore, who had long dominated the economics of tobacco planting and exports, as well as holding assembly politics in their grip, had recently faced disturbing social challenges. They kept their hold safely enough, and were able to dictate a highly conservative constitution for the new state of Maryland when the time came, but their fears of unrest at home contributed to their prolonged hesitation. Georgia, which had become a royal province only some twenty years earlier, at the instigation of a powerful faction working both in the colony and in Parliament, was now exceedingly reluctant to turn on the authority to which it looked for protection, and failed to send any delegation to the First Continental Congress. There were several individual cases of similar attitudes in other colonies, and even the Massachusetts delegation was divided during the First Congress.

The second kind of conservatism was that of men who believed in and expected reconciliation without being afflicted with the same deep-seated fear of social unrest. These might be called "confident" conservatives. They were well exemplified by most of the Virginia delegation. Such provincial potentates as Peyton Randolph or Benjamin Harrison, and men who so fully embodied the values and aspirations of the landed and slaveowning society of their province as George Washington and Edmund Pendleton, travelled to meet their colleagues at the Congress from the foundations of a self-assured ascendancy at home. No colony, perhaps, was entirely free from internal dissension. In the Carolinas, the recent Regulator troubles in the backcountry flared up again when the assemblies or conventions, dominated by the landowning classes, made the American cause their own. These disturbances were bound to cause southern leaders to glance occasionally over their shoulders. It was therefore marked evidence of their control that so few of them showed any disposition to avoid conflict with Britain out of fear for security in their own societies. Their preference for reconciliation was a matter of their general disposition toward order, their deeply ingrained loyalty to the crown, and their equally habitual (though not universal) loyalty to the Church of England. At the same time, the strength of these freely elected but highly selective oligarchs, the capability they had so long exhibited in the management of their county courts and provincial assemblies, gave them an advantage which impressed the northern delegates. There seemed no doubt about their ability to take government into their own hands if events drove them to that extremity. They had high ideas of their rights and privileges, which they felt no disposition to compromise. New Englanders, encountering these magnates for the first time, and perhaps a little apprehensive of their social eminence, were gratified to discover their warmth in the cause of American liberties.

The southern delegations had their own differences of interest, character and reputation; Richard Henry Lee who, like Henry, was a brilliant orator whose fame had reached New England, was a suspect figure with many of his fellow Virginians because it was he who had moved the inquiry, a few years earlier, into the finances of the late speaker and treasurer of the Virginia Assembly, John Robinson. That inquiry (Pendleton as executor was charged with the chief burden) had uncovered malfeasance on an enormous scale, involving many of the principal estates in the province. The great families had managed to weather the storm, but had not emerged with unscathed reputations, and were not much inclined to thank Lee for his enterprise.

## The Delegates Meet: First Decisions and Long-Term Aims

Most of the forty-five delegates who convened formally on September 5 had not met before reaching Philadelphia. Some had gained continental reputations, but most of them were not even known to each other by repute. They spent some days taking stock of each other and forming their early impressions, which in some cases quickly gave way to deeper ones. But they had enough common ground of political ideology, fortified by closely similar views of the meaning of the events of recent years, to enable them to get to know each other's opinions with very little preparation. This sense of mutual familiarity was explained not only by the simple fact that they spoke a common language, but because that language was used and understood in the same sense throughout the colonies. They read the same King James Bible (an experience, however, which does not always lead to agreed interpretations) and the same commentators on British politics and the constitution by which they all claimed to be equals. They read the same British laws, and by this time many of them would no doubt have read Blackstone's *Commentaries on the Laws of England*, which began to appear in 1765, and reached the colonies soon afterwards. More than this, their newspapers tended to carry similar, often identical, items of news from England. They thus had a stock of information about which, considering the controversial nature of the material, they shared an extraordinary degree of agreement. Even the recent American spokesmen could count on their works being read by educated men through most of the colonies. There could have been few if any men prominent enough to merit selection in a provincial delegation, who were unacquainted with the John Dickinson's *Letters of a Farmer in Pennsylvania*, which had eloquently stated the colonial case against the Townshend duties, and had been reprinted in numerous colonial papers. In Philadelphia, they were able to meet the celebrated author, and to be impressed by his scholarship, his courtesy, and, if they were perceptive, by his innate caution.[5]

Congresses were to become a regular phenomenon in American politics, but in 1774, the delegates had only the incomplete Stamp Act Congress, held in 1765 in New York, to look back on as a precedent for their proceedings. They succeeded in working together with far greater efficiency than often occurs even when much more elaborate preparations have been made. These successes were made possible by their high level of shared assumptions and agreement about the meaning of the events which had involved the colonies in their quarrels with Britain during the years since the end of the French and Indian War in 1763. Another important factor in their procedural efficiency was their long experience in conducting the proceedings of colonial assemblies. Parliamentary procedure and questions of order, as well as the organization of committees, were all known and understood in essentially the same ways by all the members. There is much evidence of disagreement between members on issues of substance, and there was an important substantial debate on how to vote, but there is little to suggest difficulties over procedure.

The first procedural decision, however, turned on matters that proved to have much substantive importance. Joseph Galloway, as speaker of the Pennsylvania Assembly, felt that it was his privilege to offer the Congress the use of the Assembly Hall, later known as the State House. But Galloway's enemies in the Pennsylvania delegation worked on other members to deflect the choice to the Carpenters' Hall. Galloway was keenly offended by this snub to his authority, and was well placed to know what it meant. He had already used his influence to exclude Charles Thomson, one of the more radical politicians in the assembly, from the Pennsylvania delegation. But in spite of his efforts, Thomson was appointed as clerk, which position gave him both a voice in the debates and the inestimable opportunity of writing the official record of the proceedings of the Congress. Thomson's method was to record only the positive results of each day's debates, so that defeated resolutions were often left out of the final record, which formed a very incomplete account of events. Both these defeats of Galloway's efforts were indications of the intense bitterness of Pennsylvania politics and ominous indications of the fate that Galloway's most ambitious designs were to meet in Congress.

Before entering into questions of policy, the members agreed to keep their deliberations secret. This was an easy decision; it was the custom of most colonial assemblies to debate in private and to publish their acts at the end of each session. Speeches in assembly were never published, and votes only rarely. The reasons for this privacy lay deep in the concept of representation in which American colonists had been schooled. Like members of Parliament they held themselves to be responsible for the public interest of the province, and just as they had a right to be protected against interference from the governor in the exercise of their duties, so they had an equal right to be shielded from encroachments on their freedom to speak their own minds on the part of their constituents. Historically, the whole of this concept of legislative privacy was in a precarious balance during this period, in both Britain and the colonies. Parliamentary debates were increasingly made public in Britain, partly because members wanted to make their own speeches known to a wider audience. In Massachusetts, the assembly had erected a gallery in 1766. But the motives behind the departure, which was instigated by Sam Adams, were precisely the kind against which members of the

Congress had good reasons for establishing their own safeguards. Adams used the gallery to get his Boston supporters to intimidate the conservative members of the House; Philadelphia itself was also teeming with radical artisans who could easily be turned into intimidating demonstrators. Pressure of this sort would not encourage free speech, but would actually inhibit many delegates from truly giving their opinions and possibly from freely representing the interests of their more distant constituents. Not all members felt confident that the obligations of secrecy would be observed. Sam Adams, a most experienced manipulator of public opinion, could be counted on to make conservative courses so unpopular as to be uncomfortable or even dangerous to those who advocated them.

The Congress could not proceed without agreement on methods of voting. Colonies had sent delegations of differing numbers, bearing no relation to their populations or the distribution of wealth. How were they to vote? At once there appeared a difference which was to have permanent constitutional significance. Delegates from wealthy and populous colonies were firmly convinced that those elements ought to be clearly reflected in the strength of the votes they carried with them to the Congress; it seemed entirely out of keeping that colonies of sparse or small populations and less wealth should have equal voting power. In this debate, Patrick Henry proclaimed that government was dissolved: "The Distinctions between Virginians, Pennsylvanians, New Yorkers and New Englanders are no more. I am not a Virginian, but an American." It was the only time that Henry said anything to disclaim his Virginian character. The effect of the scale he proposed would have been to strengthen the representation of Virginia. But the smaller colonies did not see the matter in that light. They came as independent political entities, responsible solely to their own assemblies and the people behind them. The arguments of the larger colonies would have been more effective if they had been prepared with more accurate information about the distribution of both wealth and population. But the fact soon emerged that such information had never been reliably collected. If the Congress wanted to make headway, there was no alternative but to accept the necessity, at least for the time being, of giving each colony a single vote. The decision was made with the express reservation that it was only a temporary expedient, to last until more accurate information was available. When that happened, it was expected that the whole system would be remodeled, and the equality of the individual colonies would give way to some kind of proportional representation in the two dominant elements requiring representation—first the wealth of the several colonies (probably to be estimated through taxation), and secondly their population, would be computed as a basis for voting strength in Congress. That time never arrived, because the first decision gave the smaller colonies an entrenched position which they refused to give up. It was not until the making of the federal Constitution that the proportional principle could be introduced, and even then the sovereignty of the states was retained in the Senate.

## The Massachusetts Delegation: Press for Solidarity

The sufferings of Boston inspired a spirit of self-sacrificing unity which at once encouraged the Massachusetts delegates. Alarming news of a British bombardment suddenly inflamed the local populace to an ardent state of military impatience, so that many of them seemed disappointed when the reports proved to be false. At least it gave delegates a taste of what might be in store. Some of them felt that it would be seemly to begin with prayers; but could prayers be offered up on behalf of so heterogeneous a body? After some discussion, the Congregationalist members from Massachusetts shrewdly supported an invitation to the Anglican clergyman, the Reverend Jacob Duché, who produced an extraordinary effect of unity and enthusiasm. Duché chose to read the Thirty-fifth Psalm, a well-judged call to the Lord to defend his people against his oppressors; John Adams, who had no knowledge of the Anglican service, thought the choice of psalm was a matter of chance, and suspected the hand of providence. Duché concluded the ceremony with an unexpected, extemporaneous prayer which roused the whole Congress and made a deep impression on members of very diverse persuasions. The episode was extremely helpful, and the New Englanders felt they had assisted in a shrewd move towards the militant unity they needed. Even the legions of Oliver Cromwell never felt surer that God was on their side than the inspired, though far more variegated, deputies of the American colonies.

The Massachusetts delegates, encouraged by support for beleagured Boston, reported in letters home that other colonies shared their cause. But soon they began to wonder how fully this emotional solidarity would be translated into action. Even at the very beginning, Silas Deane of Connecticut told his wife that "there are not wanting enemies to the general Cause, and who, aided by party, are restless in their endeavours to defeat or retard our proceedings."[6] Before the end of September, John Adams, who had begun with more optimism, was telling a correspondent of the fear of war; it was generally felt, he said, that Massachusetts should be patient. As for independence, or the resumption of the first Massachusetts charter—which was under discussion in the colony—these were "Ideas which Startle people here."[7]

The crisis which brought the Congress into existence arose in Massachusetts, and it was natural that the problems of that province should be uppermost. During its first few days, new events were in progress there. To avoid the parliamentary ban on town meetings, Samuel Adams and his allies arranged meetings in certain towns in Suffolk County, making them in name an action of the county rather than a town. The Suffolk Resolves, which emerged from these meetings, embodied a very full statement of colonial rights (see Document 1). While avowing allegiance to George III, they denounced the late acts of Parliament as "gross infractions of those rights to which we are justly entitled by the laws of nature, the British constitution, and the charter of the province." The Resolves recommended nonintercourse with Britain and nonconsumption of British goods, urged the encouragement of domestic manufactures, and expressed confidence in the Continental

Congress. They also sternly deplored any resort to riots against persons or property. This document was at once carried to Philadelphia by Paul Revere, who arrived on September 16, where it was debated by Congress. The tenor of the Resolves was defiant; their program was intended to carry that attitude into action; but its details remained open to debate. It was an early and important triumph for the radicals, and an enormous encouragement to the Massachusetts delegates, when the Congress agreed to approve them. John Adams told his wife that it was one of the happiest days of his life.

The Resolves, as adopted by the Congress, made economic sanctions into continental policy. They implied a determination to resist by any methods that would effect their aims. Thus at this early stage, Congress lent itself to a policy of resistance in order to achieve conciliation—through methods that could lead on to resistance even if conciliation failed. The Massachusetts radicals who engineered this demonstration had come to the Congress with ideas of American policy more advanced and clear-cut than they dared to avow. But they were not the only ones to have ideas about the future.

### The Plan of Union

No radical had thought out his plans more clearly than their most determined opponent, John Galloway. It was just as evident to Galloway as it was to anyone in the spectrum between himself and the actual separationists that the relations between Britain and her American colonies had reached an impasse which could no longer be resolved in the forms of the old relationship; he also felt that the colonies had genuine grievances which demanded redress. After delegates had spent three weeks discussing the question of the exact sources of the rights they claimed, and in particular whether the laws of nature should be invoked along with their charters and the British Constitution, Galloway rose to offer a new framework and object for the whole debate.[8] His proposal was nothing less than an original Plan of Union; for the first time, the colonies would be held together by a formal, written constitution, and this constitution would also unite them with Britain. Not since the Albany Plan (devised by Franklin in 1754) had anyone indulged in such spacious thinking about the future of the colonies. Galloway envisaged that the colonial legislatures would elect members to a "grand council" or colonial parliament; it would be presided over by a president general, appointed by the king, to hold office during his pleasure. This new parliamentary body would deal with all matters affecting more than one colony, and all those affecting relations with Britain. In all other matters, each colony would govern its own internal life. Legislation affecting America could be initiated in either the British or the American parliament, but could take effect only if agreed by both.

In an earlier debate, Galloway had argued that Americans were not subject to laws made in Britain after they had departed. This was a slightly novel version of a decidedly firm assertion of American independence from British legislative power. Yet in his opening speech on the Plan of Union, he recognized the force of the conventional theory of sovereignty; every political body must have a supreme authority, and that authority could only reside in Britain. Given this realistic appraisal of the problem, Galloway's plan was as farsighted as anything that could reasonably have been advanced at the time, in either Britain or America. He received later intimations that it might have been met by at least respectful consideration by the British ministry.

Galloway correctly foresaw that, whatever the outcome of the immediate dispute with Britain, the colonies would need to establish some form of administrative coordination of their own. His plan seems to have appealed strongly to many members of the Congress as well as to moderate reconciliationists outside, particularly in New York. He was seconded by James Duane, an enterprising New York merchant and speculator, who was to emerge later as a strong Federalist, and gained the support of John Jay, also of New York. Jay asked Colonel Lee, who had raised objections on behalf of the autonomy of the colonies, whether the plan asked them to give up one liberty or interfered with one right. Duane said that justice required that they expressly cede to Parliament the right of regulating trade. Edward Rutledge of South Carolina declared his opinion that the plan was "almost perfect." We owe our knowledge of this debate to John Adams's notes; the official *Journal* is silent, not only on the discussion (which would not have been recorded there) but on the very existence of such a proposal. This silence was the result not of neglect but of suppression.

Galloway's enemies saw the danger. If his plan went forward, and obtained British approval, then the efforts of the Congress would have resulted in making the empire both stronger and more flexible than ever before; all hope of real independence would be at an end for the indefinite future. Patrick Henry attacked the plan on the grounds that it would give to an American parliament the kind of power which had been corruptly exercised by the existing Parliament. This statement was a foretaste of the localist argument that would one day burgeon into Antifederalism. There can be little doubt that the plan's opponents were aided by the mood in which the Congress had supported the Suffolk Resolves; and the scale and novelty of Galloway's conception seems to have been too daring for the conventional thinking of many delegates, who dearly wished to be able to induce the British to go back to their old ways, leaving the colonies to run as they had in the past. This, in truth—as Galloway perceived—was now impossible. Whatever happened, the nature of the empire, and the relationship of the colonies to each other, were bound to change. But Galloway, whose social attitudes have not endeared him to later generations, and whose views are easily dismissed under the label of "conservative," was in fact offering the most advanced thinking of the time about imperial relations. That, of course, was just what the radicals understood. After an adjourned debate, they not only succeeded in dismissing the subject from the agenda, but suppressed all mention of it from the records. The ostensible aim was no doubt to present an appearance of unanimity where none existed. This remarkable example of news manipulation would have been impossible without the cooperation of the clerk, Charles Thomson. Galloway himself also blamed the timidity of his would-be supporters on outright intimidation from the streets; Samuel Adams was probably working harder outside Congress than among its members.

## Nonimportation and Nonexportation: The Colonial Association

Before Galloway introduced his plan, the Congress had already spent nearly three weeks intermittently debating the merits and consequences of banning first the import of British produce, and then the export of American produce to the British Isles. Nonimportation was much the easier matter; it had been used before, and even though the last plan, employed against the Townshend tariffs, had caused more difficulties among the colonies than it had for the British, the idea still offered the best chance of bringing colonial pressure to bear on the vulnerable points in the British system.

As was pointed out during the discussions, what the colonies wanted was not only redress, but speedy redress. The great danger was that non-importation would work too slowly to alarm the British government, which might take the alternative course of stepping up its own pressures in the meantime. The problem of a longer-term program therefore had to be faced. The records of the debates on nonconsumption, and on the much graver expedient of a ban of American exports to British ports, are unfortunately fragmentary. From the meager entries in the *Journal of the Continental Congress*, it is clear that nonimportation received formal approval as early as September 27, 1774. A committee was set to work to draw up a general plan under which the colonies, acting through the Congress, were to associate themselves, bind themselves to observe their agreements, and authorize continuing means for the enforcement of these measures. This committee's report was adopted as a formal resolution declaring the colonies' Rights and Grievances on October 14. But the difficulties were acute, and it was not until October 20, after some three weeks of debate, that the Association was concluded.

The nonimportation resolution of September 27 left a striking omission as to West Indian produce, on which the New England colonies relied for much of their carrying trade and for their domestic manufacture of molasses into sugar. Southern delegates were deeply suspicious of the intentions of New England and New York merchants; charges and insinuations of bad faith and smuggling flew from end to end of the hall. Isaac Low, a wealthy New York merchant, asserted that certain members aimed at independence and urged that the Congress adjourn for six months. The northern delegates and middle colony merchants felt obliged to concede. The Congress therefore agreed to stop the importation of molasses, coffee, and pimento from the British West Indies and Dominica, of foreign indigo, and—a heavy sacrifice—Madeira wines.

At this point, on October 6, Paul Revere made a further appearance, with alarming news that General Gage was raising fortifications in Boston. What advice could the Congress give? The more ardent members, notably Richard

Henry Lee and Gadsden, wanted a military response, and Samuel Adams drafted a fiery letter to Gage. But few members wanted to take all the risks of military engagements; it was vitally important that the ground should be left clear for their petitions and economic measures to take effect without the dangerous temper of warlike action. After five days of debate, the Congress got off a letter to Gage urging him to desist from fortifying his positions in Boston and cease permitting his forces to provoke the people. He was assured that the people of Boston would behave peaceably if only they could be assured of their own safety, a matter on which Gage's experience led him to opposite opinions. The question of whether Boston should be evacuated was returned to the Massachusetts Provincial Congress, which took no further action.

As to designs of independence, a significant social meeting took place on September 28, when George Washington, who had been warned that the New Englanders were aiming in that direction, called on the Massachusetts delegates. Samuel Adams succeeded in convincing him that they had no such intentions, to such effect that Washington told a friend that "I am as well satisfied as I can be of my existence that no such thing is desired by any thinking man in all North America." The New Englanders were not merely soft pedalling; they were concealing their deeper aims. Had Adams told Washington the truth, it is difficult to know what might have happened. Certainly the Virginians felt strongly about the threat to their own as well as to New England liberties, but on the other hand they had to reckon with the danger that New England, notorious for its disorders and republicanism, might be exploiting the high intentions of the southern colonies. The most serious danger would have been of New England's isolation. The remaining colonies, including New York, could have been persuaded that Massachusetts had brought too many of its troubles on itself and on America; it might have been left to fend for itself, with such allies as could be found elsewhere in New England. A move on these lines was actually proposed by Galloway.

More than a fortnight later, on October 13, John Adams recorded a long debate, lasting from ten in the morning until half past four, on the power of Parliament to regulate trade. Even his own delegation was divided on this issue. The difficulties were genuine. Unless the colonies were actually to cast off all parliamentary power, then they must admit that it existed in certain cases, and the general interests of the British Empire, as opposed to the French, Spanish and Portuguese empires, were the area in which the colonies had been traditionally prepared to admit the ascendancy of Parliament. This view conceded that Parliament would retain its authority in war and peace; it meant that Parliament might levy such duties as were required for the regulation of the flow of merchandise, though not in order to raise a revenue.

These views actually appeared in the resolutions of October 14. Their form, proposed by John Adams as a way of breaking a serious deadlock which found the delegations almost equally divided, gave little satisfaction to either side. It declared that, since the colonies were not and could not be represented in Parliament, they were entitled to the exclusive right of legislation over all matters of taxation and internal policy, allowing for the royal power of veto. "But," it was added, "from the necessity of the case . . . we cheerfully consent to the operation of such acts of the British Parliament, as are bona fide, restrained to the regulation of our external commerce, for the purpose of securing the commercial advantages of the whole empire to the mother country, and the commercial benefits of its representative members; excluding every idea of taxation, internal or external, for raising a revenue on the subjects in America, without their consent."[9] This was a concession that radicals were reluctant to make. They were better satisfied with a reference to the laws of nature as being among the foundations of their rights, included in a preamble to the resolutions. The division here was between those who were content to rely on the laws of England and the charters, and those who wanted to invoke natural law as being higher than any right that the colonists claimed from England. It was not, as might be thought, a difference between lawyers and popular propagandists, but again between conservatives and radicals on the basic connection with Britain. John Adams, a lawyer, and in domestic politics a conservative, wanted the appeal to the laws of nature. From the tactical point of view, it enabled the Americans to outflank any argument that might be sprung from the highly debatable meaning of English constitutional law. We do not know by what arguments the more radical members managed to gain a majority; there was certainly a spirited discussion, but perhaps some of those who found the legal arguments troublesome or inconclusive felt that one additional American claim could do them no harm and might prove useful if they ran out of legal arguments later on.

The Association itself was the most important outcome of the First Continental Congress (see Document 1-b). In recalling the offenses under which Americans had suffered, it dated British aggressions from "about the year 1763." South Carolina delegates had wanted to go further back, claiming that previous parliamentary regulations were unlawful in the colonies. The choice of the year 1763, however, had the advantage of pointing the accusation at George III and his unpopular ministers. It had a further concealed advantage for the holders or claimants of land grants made by the crown before 1763. By far the most extensive of these were claimed by Virginia, whose vast domain reached far into the Ohio Valley. Conflicts over western land claims erupted even before the Second Congress had reached the point of independence; they troubled the relations between the states during the ensuing war, and held up the signing of the Articles of Confederation.

Two features of the Association reflected the divisions that lay behind it. The first, in order, was the timetable for continental action. The agreement on nonimportation, which was the least contentious, was to go into effect against Great Britain, Ireland, and the British West Indies, on December 1, 1774. The next stage was nonconsumption of British products, which was set for March 1, by which time all British imports ordered before the ban were expected to have been consumed.

Nonexportation, however, was agreed to only after a dispute on which the whole Congress nearly foundered. The argument began on September 26, when Thomas Cushing of Massachusetts moved that all three measures—nonimportation, nonconsumption and nonexportation—should begin at once. The Virginians, however, were under instructions not to agree to non-exportation until August 10, 1775, by which time their tobacco crop of 1774 would have been cured and marketed. They even urged the autumn of 1776 as a more appropriate period for this ban. Northern colonies objected that they, too, had goods which were exported in the year after they had been produced. Edward Rutledge of South Carolina suggested that Virginians should raise wheat instead of tobacco (many of them, as a matter of fact, raised it along with tobacco.) But South Carolina—represented significantly by its tidewater planters, not its backcountry farmers—was equally determined to protect its rice exports. In the end, South Carolina refused to sign unless rice exports were exempted.[10] When they got home, that colony's delegates faced bitter protests for having protected these tidewater interests to the neglect of all the produce of the interior. The Virginia date, September 10, 1775, was finally agreed for the beginning of nonexportation. One further decision, on which there is a disappointing lack of clarifying contemporary comment, was to forbid the importation of slaves. In view of the foreign exchange problems seen to face the Americans, this policy may well have had economic imperatives behind it; but Virginia had in any case tried to stabilize its racial composition by stopping slave imports, only to have this disallowed by the crown a few years earlier. The Association also proclaimed the intention of its adherents to promote frugality, to renounce extravagent ceremonies, and to encourage the breeding of sheep and the manufacture of American goods. These plans would provide domestic alternatives to British imports, and were indispensable to either of the alternatives that lay ahead—pressure on Britain through economic sanctions, or independence through war.

## Effects of the First Congress

In trying to understand the seemingly slow progress of the American colonies towards independence, these difficulties and this timetable of economic action are extremely important. Five months before the nonexport agreement was due to begin, war had broken out. Yet Americans could still hope that the combined effects of their economic restrictions and military operations would induce the British to make more reasonable terms. When we reflect that the Virginian delegates, who certainly included some militant patriots, were under instructions to suggest the fall of 1776 as a time for implementing that side of the plan, and given that unanimity was indispensable to the success of the colonial cause, it becomes easier to understand the pace with which the colonies, acting as they had to do through the lengthy and deliberative processes of the Congress, moved as a whole towards independence. The impatient New Englanders, while expressing their exasperation in letters home, could only bide their time, and hope that the British would stubbornly refuse to see reason. On that point at least they had the comfort of the king's cooperation.

The Association also included provisions for the enforcement of its policies through a series of local committees, to be elected by existing electorates. These were the first official steps towards the coercion of the recalcitrant minorities. Noncooperators were to be posted as enemies of the American people, and would obviously be deprived of the normal forms of protection. The threat was not to be taken lightly. Tarring and feathering was an appalling torture which victims did not always survive; other forms of persecution could deprive people of their livings, perhaps of their homes. One Charlestonian was reported as turning white on merely receiving a letter from his local committee.

During the preceding weeks the Congress had debated a series of addresses, which it now formally approved. The king had to be petitioned once again with the familiar protestations of loyalty and the familiar list of grievances. But the people of Great Britain were also appealed to, at considerable length. The Congress dwelt heavily on the community of their forebears, principles and rights which ought to bring the British people to their side. They did not fail to mention the common inheritance of the Protestant religion, now menaced by the Quebec Act, which recognized the Roman Catholic establishment of the French Canadians. Similarly, in addressing the people of the colonies, the Congress warned of the danger to their religious freedom. The Catholic religion was well understood by Protestants as a potent instrument of tyranny, and its approval by George III and his ministers could only be taken in that sense. But it was also necessary, for strategic reasons, to try to gain the confidence of the Canadians. In drawing up its address to them, the Congress treated their religious susceptibilities with greater respect. They were told that they had everything to gain from a union with the American colonies, for their liberties would in turn be threatened by the same British government.

Before dissolving, the Congress provided for the election of a second Congress, to meet in May, 1775, if the redress sought for had not been provided. The petitions were in fact treated with contempt by the king and his ministers; Benjamin Franklin, waiting on Lord Hillsborough, the secretary of state for the colonies, could not even gain admittance. This treatment meant that the acts of the Congress, and in particular the Association, became the forerunners of a further Congress, devoted to military preparations and civil war. In that light, the measures of September and October, 1774, clearly emerge as the first steps towards independence. But the majority neither hoped nor intended that they should be taken to bear that meaning either among the colonies or in Britain. It should be noted that their preparations excluded anything of a military nature. The more militant plans for the defense of Boston, along with a motion by Richard Henry Lee, to order the mobilization of militia forces, were all defeated.

On October 27, Dickinson wrote to Arthur Lee in London that Congress had broken up yesterday. The colonists, he said, had taken such ground that

Great Britain must relax, or involve herself in civil war. He emphasized the determination of the colonies, expressed his own ardent wish for peace, but added that "the first act of violence from Administration in America will put the whole continent in arms." So would an attempt to reinforce Gage's troops in Boston during the coming winter or the following year. Dickinson, whose timidity had already been observed by John Adams, was never to be quite so militant again. But this bold, if private, letter was a manifestation of the confidence the colonial delegates had gained from each others' company and resolution and from the agreements they had made.

In retrospect, the First Continental Congress can be seen as having initiated a series. It was followed by the Second Congress, which adjourned only to reconvene and launch the War of Independence and proclaim the independence of the United States. Since that time the United States has been governed by congresses, under the Articles of Confederation—formed during the war years by the Continental Congress itself—and subsequently under the Constitution. Because of the ease with which this familiar retrospect suggests the intentions of the members themselves, it is particularly important to recall that for most of the delegates these events were not in their plans, still less in their hopes. The reason why the First Congress inaugurated a series is that it failed in its primary aims. The avowed purpose of the majority was to achieve a full reconciliation with Great Britain, on terms that would recognize the autonomy of the American colonies in matters purely internal to themselves, while probably leaving to Parliament some broad, not fully defined powers over the empire as a whole. The details were never worked out because neither Parliament nor the king was willing to make any satisfactory gesture of response. This refusal threw the Congress back onto its own longer-term plan of bringing pressure to bear on Britain by withdrawing American trade. Some members welcomed British intransigence; it forced the conservatives into the adoption of more radical policies. But for the majority of members, this necessity was the result of failure, not success.

## Notes

1. *The Letters of a Farmer in Pennsylvania to the Inhabitants of the British Colonies* began to appear in the Philadelphia newspapers in November 1767 and rapidly became the most widely read and generally accepted statement of the colonial cause. Their author, though anonymous, did not long remain unidentified.

2. Peter Kalm, *Travels into North America*, trans. J. R. Forster, 3 vols. (Warrington, England, 1770-71), vol. 1, p. 265.

3. Alfred E. Young, *The Democratic Republicans of New York, 1763-1797* (Chapel Hill: University of North Carolina Press, 1967), p. 15.

4. Ibid., p. 12.

5. Dickinson appeared in Congress on October 17, after the. radicals had succeeded in adding his name to the list of Pennsylvania delegates—a setback for his old enemy, Galloway.

6. Edmund C. Burnett, ed., *Letters of Members of the Continental Congress* (Washington, D.C.: The Carnegie Institution, 1921), vol. 1, pp. 4-5.

7. Ibid., p. 48.

8. For information on Galloway, see Julian P. Boyd, ed., *Anglo-American Union: Joseph Galloways's Plans to Preserve the British Empire, 1744-1788* (Philadelphia: University of Pennsylvania Press, 1941); and Benjamin H. Newcomb, *Franklin and Galloway: A Political Partnership* (New Haven and London: Yale University Press, 1972).

9. Merrill Jensen, ed., *English Historical Documents* (London and New York: Spottiswoode, 1955), vol. 9, pp. 806-7.

10. From the notes of the debate by John Adams, in L. H. Butterfield et al., eds., *The Diary of John Adams* (Cambridge: Harvard University Press, 1961), vol. 2, pp. 137-38.

# 2

## Winter in the Provinces, 1774-1775

### Militancy and Indecision: Obstacles to Action

When the Continental Congress met, power had already begun to pass from the hands of the royal authorities and constitutional assemblies into those of extra-legal conventions and committees. Each colony managed and timed this transformation in its own way. The necessity for conventions arose, however, from one common condition: precisely because they had no foundation in the existing colonial constitutions, they lay wholly outside the powers of royal or proprietary governors. A governor could dissolve an assembly, but he could not touch a convention. The use of the same election laws as applied to assembly elections gave the conventions a strong foundation in the appearances, if not the facts, of legality, which was important to people whose claims rested on their charters and on the British constitution. When the Continental Congress adopted the Association and in turn recommended it to the several colonies, it offered them a set of common principles and a method of collective action. What followed, however, would depend entirely on two other factors. The first and most immediate was the response of people of the colonies; the second was the attitude of British government.

The progressive breakdown of the formal structure of power threw unprecedented opportunities into the hands of local militants. The radical activists who formed the local committees, enforced the recommendations of the Congress, and frequently reached far beyond them to insist on conformity to their own views of the requirements of patriotic policy, naturally acted in the name of the people. In many places, they clearly had the acquiescence and often the support of large majorities; but the violence which they used to menace recalcitrants, to force merchants to obey the nonimportation decrees, and to intimidate people into signing the Association—used in Virginia as a sort of loyalty oath—strongly suggests that they were aware of the latent dangers from opposition and indifference.

The intense activism of these elements, and their successes in a wide variety of colonies, including most of New England, Pennsylvania, Maryland,

Virginia, and South Carolina, strongly suggested that in fact the people were ready to support local leaders whose militancy was far in advance of the Continental Congress itself. During the winter of 1774-1775, eight colonies made provisions through their conventions for raising forces to oppose British regiments, if force should be used. It is impossible to define the attitude of these very widespread prospective or active militants to the ultimate question of independence. They believed their existing liberties were gravely threatened, and in certain cases they also believed that they could work changes in the structure of domestic government; a period of crisis could be turned into a period of social change. But the question of independence was fraught with uncertainties. In the Carolinas, it would mean placing all the power in the assemblies that were already dominated by seaboard interests distrusted by the interior; many backcountry farmers had no desire to divest themselves of the British monarchy as an ultimate court of appeal against their powerful provincial magnates. Even in Massachusetts, the advance of the crisis revealed the presence of articulate and courageous people who were not prepared to be browbeaten into submission by the mobs of Boston or the activists of their own towns.

The winter thus brought very ambiguous developments. It certainly advanced the actual grip of those elements who were willing to defy the British even with arms; but in the process it revealed the depth of the divisions within American society. While the southern colonies of Maryland, Virginia and South Carolina enforced the Association, North Carolina remained divided and hesitant, and Georgia was positively unwilling to move. New Jersey, with Quaker elements lying outside of Philadelphia, and deeply conservative merchants on the Hudson, was a divided and indecisive province. While the local committee of Philadelphia energetically enforced the Association by a boycott of British imports, in January 1775 the Quakers of the city issued a statement denouncing "all combinations, insurrections, conspiracies and illegal assemblages," and showed no reticence in their hostility to measures that infringed on the activities of commerce or threatened to worsen the quarrel with Britain. In February, Joseph Galloway took his seat in the reconvened assembly to renew his struggle against the acts of the Continental Congress, and won an impressive initial success; for a short time it looked as though Pennsylvania was swinging away from the policies of the Congress and might unhinge the whole Association. Then a committee that had been told to draft a report along Galloway's lines gave way to radical influences and brought in a report contrary to its instructions. Galloway was preparing another report while this particular coup was brought about, and though he denounced it with understandable bitterness, he could not reverse it; the assembly majority now moved behind its committee. Galloway's loyalism, coupled with his personal unpopularity and his defeat at the hands of political enemies who eventually identified themselves as patriots, have obscured the courage and tenacity of his fight for the constitutional position in which he believed. After his last defeat he sailed for England, and was never allowed to return; much of the information available about events in

Pennsylvania comes from his evidence to the inquiry of the House of Commons into American affairs, and from his own subsequent writings.[1] But it was a cruel irony for him that he was very largely trapped, not so much by the conflict over the great imperial crisis, but by the party rivalry which had for years set him against Dickinson. After Galloway's defeat, it was Dickinson who emerged, not only in his own province but in the Congress itself, no longer as the brilliant champion of American rights, but as the most influential and tactically shrewdest opponent of all measures tending to independence. Dickinson carried this extreme defensive caution with him back into the Second Continental Congress.

Even Massachusetts gave unexpected signs of conservative vitality. A wealthy lawyer, Daniel Leonard, writing under the name of "Massachusettensis", fiercely attacked the illegal doings of the Congress and accused it of aiming at independence; and at this stage John Adams, replying as "Novanglus", thought it expedient to deny that charge. Meanwhile, people who refused to conform to the majority were forced to leave their homes in rural towns, and fled in large numbers to the protection of Boston, where there was at least a British regiment. Even the leaders of Boston, however, began to be alarmed at the imminent threat of warfare. The populace had too often been excited to fever pitch. In the countryside, the farmers seemed to be itching to get out their guns and drive the army out once and for all. It was when Gage began to build fortifications against this threat that the Boston committee of correspondence sent for advice to the Continental Congress, hoping for something to allay the excitement; Congress's cautious recommendation not to evacuate the town was in fact the best news Boston could get. Suspicion against merchants thought to be harboring imported goods for later sale made the internal situation there still more uneasy. If open fighting broke out, there could be no certainty that the other colonies would rush to Boston's aid. Samuel Adams, who declared that they would, was called a liar by his colleague Thomas Cushing, who said Adams knew they would not. In this dangerous passage through the winter, General Gage was well aware of the risks, and did everything to avert an outbreak. On neither side, for the moment, did the leadership want to take that step.

The greatest obstacle to American action lay in New York, whose assembly was now in the influence of the great De Lancey family, which had temporarily choked its rivals, the Livingstons, out of power. The assembly refused to thank the colony's delegates when they returned from Philadelphia. Only three of New York's thirteen counties responded favorably to the Association, and seven ignored it. In the spring of 1775 the assembly, still under De Lancey leadership, refused even to send delegates to the Second Continental Congress, with the result that delegates appeared there in a desultory way from individual counties.

The De Lanceys meanwhile took an initiative that indicated their total rejection of continental political action. Instead of joining the Association, they led the assembly in its own petitions to both Houses of Parliament in England. Both rejected these petitions. This, following the British rejection of the addresses of the Continental Congress, constituted an ominous sign of the way the ultimate determinant was going to work. Lord North's administration failed to offer the American loyalists and moderates the gesture they needed in order to keep their own policy alive. The moderates, who included many later Whigs, could probably have prevailed, and could certainly have prevented anything like united colonial action, if they had received a serious offer of British support.

## Lexington and Concord:  The First American Resistance

Lord North had other plans. Early in 1775 he prepared a bill to restrain the commerce of New England. Then, as much to deflate the opposition in Parliament as to help the Americans, he introduced a motion on reconciliation, which came to be known as his olive branch (see Document 2). It was not of the sort that could appease American opinion after the session of the Continental Congress. The proposal was that Parliament would desist from levying taxes on any colony which raised its own and handed the proceeds over to Parliament for disposal; the colonial assemblies were also to provide for the support of civil government. Charles Fox and Edmund Burke in the House of Commons, and Chatham in the House of Lords, scornfully denounced this resolution as a sham and a mockery, which the Americans would spurn. The effect on American opinion was worse than useless, because it suggested that the British—as Fox charged—were insincere in professions of desire for peace. Its arrival was also unfortunately timed, coinciding with the news of the fighting at Lexington and Concord.

Meanwhile, however, the nonimportation agreement was working with remarkable effect. Statistics suggest that the value of imports from Britain dropped in 1775 by no less than ninety-seven percent below the level of 1774. If this effort could be maintained, then moderates could reasonably hope that Britain would be forced to make concessions. Even if conflict could not be averted, it might still be contained to the level of a holding operation while Britain took time to reconsider.

In Virginia, Peyton Randolph, who had been given the authority to call a new convention, acted in the interests of moderation by delaying that step as long as he safely could against the popular groundswell. When delegates were at last called, and assembled in Richmond on March 20, they began thanking their governor, Lord Dunmore, for his recent service in a war against the Indians. Dunmore had done the Virginians his last service, however; almost at once he issued a proclamation, following a recent British order, under which the land grant system in the colony's vacant areas was radically changed. In future, the costs were to be met at public auctions and the lands for sale were to be designated by surveys. This came as a severe shock to many powerful and ambitious men, and worse followed when Dunmore disallowed patents issued under a proclamation of 1754 because the surveyor had not been qualified. George Washington, who held immense tracts under these patents, could hardly believe the news. Nothing could have done more at that moment to convince the magnates of Virginia that their future would be safer in their own hands than in the king's. It seems reasonable to take this as a point at which the psychology necessary to independence was brought to life by the calculation of rational self-interest. Neither Washington, Randolph, nor many others had been of that frame of mind the previous fall.

Patrick Henry meanwhile moved that the colony be placed in a state of defense. His celebrated speech[2], the preservation or reconstruction of which we owe to his biographer William Wirt, evoked in his hearers a familiar passage from Jeremiah:[3]

> Gentlemen may cry peace, peace—but there is no peace. The war is actually begun! The next gale that sweeps from the North will bring to our ears the clash of resounding arms! Our brethren are already in the field! Why stand we here idle! What is it that gentlemen wish? What would they have? Is life so dear or peace so sweet that they are to be purchased at the price of chains and slavery? Forbid it, Almighty God—I know not what course others may take, but as for me, give me liberty or give me death!

Henry himself was soon in the field, and Lord Dunmore in a state of armed defense. But Henry's statement was a little in advance of events. It was not until April 19, in Massachusetts, that General Gage, sending a body of troops to collect the arms from the armory at Concord, encountered the first positive American resistance. The farmers who had waited with such impatience now formed with the celerity of trained soldiers. The firing started when the column reached Lexington and burst out again at Concord bridge; the British column was severely mauled before it scrambled back to Boston. Despite their own losses, the people of Massachusetts could feel that they had shown the British that every inch of ground would be contested if it came to war. The gales that swept from the North soon brought the news to the delegates of the Second Continental Congress, and gave them a new agenda. At the first Congress, the exigencies of British pressure were still contained by the forms of law, and called only for civil responses. But now Congress had to prepare for war. The facts of the case as they met had sharply diminished the possibilities of conciliation.

## Notes

1.  *The Examination of Joseph Galloway, Esq., Late Speaker of the House of Assembly of Pennsylvania, Before the House of Commons* (London, 1779); Joseph Galloway, *Reflections on the Rise and Progress of the American Rebellion* (London, 1780).

2.  See William Wirt, *The Life of Patrick Henry* (New York, 1831), pp. 137-41. There are discussions of sources based on contemporary recollections in Moses Coit Tyler, *Patrick Henry* (New York, 1889), pp. 145-51, and in Robert Douthat Meade, *Patrick Henry, Practical Revolutionary* (Philadelphia: J. B. Lippincott Co., 1969), chapter 3.

3.  Jer. 6:14. This reference seems to me to bear favorably on the authenticity of the passage.

# 3

## Lord North Defines the Alternatives

### British Measures Against Rebellion

Whatever course others might take, the outcome for America was bound to depend on the attitude of the British administration.[1] That attitude was an embodiment of the opinions of Lord North, who since 1770 had held the position equivalent to that of the modern prime minister, and of a small circle of ministers including William Legge, Earl of Dartmouth, who became secretary for the American colonies in August 1772—and finally of the king himself. The most important fact about this ministry was its strength. For some seven previous years, the young but exceedingly serious-minded king had floundered in his attempts to find ministers who could command sufficient influence in the House of Commons while remaining loyal to himself. In Lord North he found a minister who held at least a reasonable degree of respect among members of Parliament, and whose views were reassuringly close to his own. The stubborn attitudes of British government, their imperviousness to criticism inside or outside Parliament, sprang in large measure from the inner confidence of king and ministers in themselves and each other. North was easily able to get the backing of a consistently large majority in the House of Commons, not because members were bribed or pensioned, but because his policies reflected their own prejudices, and because in general, and especially in difficult times, they believed that the king's government ought to be supported.

Americans hoping for reconciliation during the summer of 1774 counted much too heavily on the political power of the emergent radical movement in England.[2] It was true that John Wilkes had rallied an encouraging show of strength only a few years earlier, and that radical societies were forming, especially in London; but they had no national constituency. The political public was not yet attuned to making the connections which seemed so obvious to Americans, between the ministry's punitive measures in the colonies and their repressive outbursts at home. Since about 1769, British radicals had been publishing pamphlets and exerting themselves in particular elections, but they had heavy work in promoting the American cause; the destruction of the tea in Boston Harbor was not an act that could easily be defended in Britain, and lost rather than gained British friends for the Bostonians. Most people probably agreed that the tea ought to be paid for. Not much had happened to change these feelings by the time the First Continental Congress met. In September, 1774, perhaps to forestall any possible change in sentiment, George III suddenly dissolved Parliament.

The ensuing general election produced no significant change in the composition of the House of Commons. On opening the new Parliament in December, the king condemned the new nonimportation movement, alluded to a "most daring spirit of resistance and disobedience to law" rampant in Massachusetts and announced his "firm and steadfast resolution to withstand every attempt to weaken or impair the supreme authority of the Legislature over all the dominions of the Crown." This, of course, was an assertion of parliamentary as well as royal power. In February, 1775, after examining the American papers in the ministry's possession, Parliament agreed with Lord North that a rebellion existed in Massachusetts, encouraged by illegal combinations in several other colonies.

There was little that the opposition could do. Burke delivered his famous speech on American taxation in April, 1774; but he reviewed the record of the American quarrel as a partisan of Lord Rockingham, whose administration had repealed the Stamp Act but passed the Declaratory Act. Burke, therefore, was basically committed to the view that Parliament possessed and must retain an ultimate constitutional power to legislate for the colonies. His differences with the administration were of management and common sense. The situation was much worse when he delivered a speech on Conciliation with the Colonies in March, 1775. Burke could see no sense in sticking to legalistically defined powers or rights when wisdom and moderation could lead both sides to an accommodation which was in the true interests of both. He saw the conflict as supremely unnecessary, a result of shallow and ignorant self-righteousness; and he understood the temper of the colonies far more clearly than did the ministry or their majority. He also understood the weakness at the heart of the administration's show of strength: "First, Sir, permit me to observe that the use of force alone is but *temporary*," he told the House of Commons. "It may subdue for a moment, but it does not remove the necessity of subduing again; and a nation is not governed which is perpetually to be conquered."[3] But the motion at the end of this famous speech lost by 78 votes to 270—in a House that was seldom forced to a division. If Burke and his colleagues had prevailed, they could certainly have produced a rational policy which would have made the radical American remedies pointless; the American conservatism that held out for so long to prevent headlong measures in Congress would then have been vindicated. It is doubtful whether such men as Samuel Adams would have been grateful. The empire would have been saved; but the colonial radicals would have been frustrated.

But early in 1775 the administration decided to impose order in the colonies. Gage had warned them that his forces were weak. He told Lord

Barrington, secretary of war, "If you think ten thousand men sufficient, send twenty; if one million is thought enough, give two; you will save both blood and treasure in the end. A large force will terrify, and engage many to join you, a middling one will encourage resistance and gain no friends."[4] This shrewd advice was ignored and the ministry dispatched only two infantry regiments, one cavalry, and six hundred more marines. Three major generals, John Burgoyne, Sir Henry Clinton, and William Howe were sent to reinforce Gage—in effect to take over from him. They reached Boston late in May. Dartmouth urged that commissioners be sent to compose the differences with the colonists, but this conciliatory advice was rejected in favor of North's olive branch (see Document 2). The Second Continental Congress assembled to hear of a peace offer, which carried no credibility, and the news of bloodshed at Lexington and Concord.

## Congress Goes to War and Assumes Powers of Government

Unlike its predecessor, the new Congress thus faced a military emergency. After examining depositions describing the actions at Lexington and Concord, Congress resolved, on May 26, to place the colonies in a state of defense. It also turned its attention to the need to provide against an invasion from Quebec and to prevent the British from severing land communications between New York City and the rest of the province. The New York authorities were ordered to take possession of the high ground overlooking the Hudson River. The Congress also composed a letter of blandishments to the people of Canada, and appointed a committee, with Colonel Washington as a member, to concern itself with ammunition and military supplies.

In order to go to the aid of Boston and fulfill its other obligations against regular British forces, the Congress had to raise a continental army. Military command, supplies, and pay were all essential matters of policy, which could be provided for only after senior officers had been appointed. The first problem was to find a commander in chief. Probably the most distinguished military reputations in the colonies were those of Israel Putnam of Connecticut and Charles Lee of Virginia. But George Washington, who had won luster as a militia colonel during the rout of General Braddock's regulars twenty years earlier, was also a strong candidate, and had been dropping a broad hint to his colleagues by turning up in Congress in his militia uniform. The northern colonies would have preferred Putnam; if he had been chosen, much of the nomenclature of American history and topography would certainly have been different. But there were cogent political reasons for turning to Virginia. The Adamses were sufficiently conscious of the danger that a continental army, operating around Boston under a northern commander, might fail to carry the support of other colonies. Preferring Washington to Lee, perhaps on grounds of character, John Adams made the speech of nomination for the high command, in the course of which he took advantage of the opportunity to mortify his conceited Boston colleague John Hancock, who expected the command for himself. Hancock, sitting as president of the Congress, listened with glowing attention as Adams enlarged on the merits of the candidate he was about to name. Then Adams named Washington; Hancock's face darkened, and Adams was never completely forgiven.

The other generals had to be appointed with careful regard to the services and sensitivities of the various colonies. Geographical considerations sometimes prevailed over merit, and men fought for the distinction of military rank with a determination that would have earned them greater fame in the field of battle.

Before Washington departed to take up his command, Massachusetts forces were already in action. On June 12, Gage decided to occupy high ground outside Boston, and the Boston Committee of Safety at once decided to meet the threat by taking Bunker Hill. The troops actually dug their main positions on Breed's Hill, a lower and more vulnerable position, and it was there that the main action followed. The British, repeating in war the error of underestimating the Americans that they had already made in politics, exposed themselves to the exceptionally accurate fire of the Massachusetts farmers, and suffered unexpectedly high losses; the farmers had dug entrenchments and held their ground under terrific pressure. When at length they retired, General Howe let them go, despite Clinton's plea for pursuit. The British, whose nearest reinforcements might take three months to arrive, could not afford many more such victories. But the Americans had also suffered severely, particularly in the death of Joseph Warren, who would almost certainly have come forward as a leader of national importance.

The news reached Congress on June 22. On that day, it took a step that was indispensable to support its military obligations and which at the same time committed it to one of the definitive characteristics of an independent government. This was the decision to emit two million dollars in paper money. In the eighteenth century, paper money did not circulate freely, but had to be made good by specific, dated promises of redemption. If people were to accept the Congress's money as currency, they were required to believe that Congress would be able to redeem its promises; if the American cause failed, and the Congress collapsed, the value of the money would be wiped out. During the following month the delegates debated how to raise the required funds, and determined late in July that each colony must contribute its own share of the bills emitted by Congress; proportions were to be based on numbers of inhabitants of all ages. This meant that in requisitions, as for voting, the population was to form the basis of assessment; it was a necessity of the situation rather than a commitment to principles of personal equality, but it did have the long-term effect of building political individuality into the foundations of the American system of government.

As the months passed, Congress made further and more detailed provisions for the emission of currency. It would soon embark on the complex courses of raising subscriptions in America and of negotiating for loans in France and the Netherlands. Its bills quickly began to depreciate, which for the time being only meant larger and larger issues.

In providing for the army the Congress at once encountered the tricky problems of soldiers' and officers' pay. The Congress decided to pay major generals $160 a month, brigadier generals $125 a month, captains $20 a month and so forth down to private soldiers at $6.67 a month. These differentials brought sharply to the surface the fact that the colonies made differing assumptions about social rank; turned into pecuniary reward, they were divisive. John Adams was later warned by Joseph Hawley of Northampton, Massachusetts, that the army would not last the winter if the private soldiers were not given more encouragement. Adams replied that all the gentlemen from the South thought the pay of the privates too high and that of the officers too low. "Gentlemen of sense or any kind of education" he explained "are much fewer in the other colonies than in New England. They have large plantations of slaves and the common people are very ignorant and poor."[5] The gentlemen in consequence had high notions of themselves. The winter was yet young when Washington's army did in fact show signs of disintegration, but this aspect of its rewards for service got little encouragement from Congress. This problem did not bear directly on the ultimate probability or timing of American independence; it did show that the New Englanders, who had the most urgent need for help were obliged to make ideologically disagreeable concessions for the sake of unity. Sacrifices from many sides would cut deeper as the war advanced. In making these sacrifices the colonies delegated powers that gave to the Congress more of the attributes of a continental government, and took it closer to the substance of independence.

## Justifying Armed Resistance

It has always to be borne in mind that the Congress continued to deliberate in secrecy, publishing only such resolutions and announcements as it thought the public needed to know; the peoples of different colonies could follow events as reported in the papers, but gained only limited access to the proceedings by which their own representatives were making their future. The decision to raise an army made military and political problems inseparable; it had first to be justified to the American people themselves. On behalf of the Congress, Thomas Jefferson, who had recently arrived from Virginia to take the place of the ailing Peyton Randolph, drafted a provisional statement of the reasons for taking up arms. This draft was far too aggressive for the anxious taste of Dickinson, whose standing was so high that it was agreed to let him rewrite the document.

The Declaration of the Causes of Taking Up Arms as finally approved was a curiously mixed piece of rhetoric (see Document 3). It rehearsed the wrongs inflicted on America, now compounded by cruel violence and the shedding of innocent blood, but concluded with a pious hope that God, designated as "the supreme and impartial Judge and Ruler of the Universe", would "dispose our adversaries to reconciliation on reasonable terms, and thereby relieve the Empire from the calamities of civil war." This declaration followed immediately on a resolution by which the Congress proclaimed that the acts of Parliament restraining the trade of the colonies were "unconstitutional, oppressive and cruel." But Dickinson used his influence to insist that these assertions by the colonists of their determination to fight for their rights must be accompanied by still further petitions to awaken the consciences of the king and his people. According to Jefferson, the Address to the People of Great Britain was agreed upon mainly to please Dickinson, who wrote most of it. John Adams intensely disliked it; it was full, he told James Warren, of "Prettynesses, Juvenilities and Puerilities" which did not become" a great assembly like this the Representative of a great People."[6] He also said that a day and a half had been spent debating whether to call the Declaration of Causes a "declaration" or a "manifesto." It is clear that the demands of secrecy were imposing a strain on some of the delegates. John Adams's letters during July slipped many broad hints as to events and individuals, but the broadest of them rebounded to damage his own influence. "I am determined to write freely to you, this time," he told James Warren on July 24; "A certain great Fortune and piddling Genius, whose Fame has been trumpeted so loudly, has given a silly Cast to our whole Doings. We are between Hawk and Buzzard."[7] The letter became known to the British, who made sure that it was published. Dickinson, the unmistakable object of Adams's contempt, was bitterly offended, and soon afterwards cut Adams in the street in Philadelphia.

Adams could never understand the feelings of the people whose deepest desire was to have America's grievances freely and fairly set right, not in order to affirm the autonomy of the colonies, but in order to remain within the orbit of the British Empire (see Document 3-a). He wrote to his wife and others at home describing with dismay the alternating and contradictory attitudes of colleagues who veered from defiance to a posture of pleading remonstrance that filled him with disgust. His own attitudes were partly derived from the historical experience of his region—his country, as people called their colonies—and partly from his own personality. New England had always been more separate in thought and religion, more conscious of itself not merely as a colonial extension of England but as a new, positive, and superior moral foundation, than the other colonized regions of either continental America or the West Indies. The attitude had not been consistently translated into policy; it had in fact been materially supplanted when William and Mary imposed a new charter on Massachusetts after the Glorious Revolution; but it had never disappeared. John Adams himself, with all his impressive abilities, his command of business, wide-ranging knowledge of law and history, and powers of formal exposition, was in some ways an indifferent judge of political tactics. Profoundly consistent and intensely loyal, he was a far more honest man and a far less effective tactician than his cousin. He spoke too strenuously and too often; in his incessant hammering for steps that would make for independence simply because they would be irreversible, he probably did his cause more harm than good, and may well have accounted for some of the reactions that he found so distressingly difficult to explain. He seems to have been blunt rather than tactful; his feelings about Dickinson can hardly have been well concealed even before the disastrous exposure. But his powers of mind and intensity of purpose could not be denied. When independence finally arrived, he could truly claim to have been there long before.

Dickinson, who had made his name by expounding the colonial cause in reply to the Townshend tariffs, now appeared inconsistent. But his attitude in the Congress actually drew upon a deep personal consistency. The *Farmer's Letters* developed a very strong case for colonial exemption from parliamentary taxation and of ordinary legislation; but they came nowhere near to a case for colonial independence. His most earnest hope was to avert separation: "Torn from the body, to which we are united by religion, liberty, laws, affections, relation, language and commerce, we must bleed at every vein." It would have been hard to choose more graphic language to describe the ties of blood, culture, religion, and natural affection. With Galloway, his hated political enemy, defeated for personal rather than ideological reasons, Dickinson was free to assume his true role as the colonies' most persuasive spokesman for fair conciliation. His personality differed from John Adams's in a lacking certain vital boldness and determination. Dickinson was genuinely cautious and temperamentally preferred the conciliated agreement to the imposed decision.

His old Pennsylvania enemy Franklin was now thinking his way towards independence. He saw clearly that the colonies would need a more effective framework than the makeshift authority of the Continental Congress, and presented a preliminary plan for articles of confederation. But Franklin also left the door open for a restoration of British goodwill, and proposed only that his plan should remain in force until reconciliation with Britain had been effected and the offensive acts repealed. If these hopes were disappointed, the mere fact that articles had been adopted would obviously give the colonies more strength. But Franklin's plan was not taken up. The Congress was busy with a reply to Lord North's conciliatory proposition, with preparing an address to the speaker and assembly of Jamaica, authorizing a further issue of bills up to one million dollars, and establishing its own postmaster general. This office would eventually supersede that of the British-appointed postmaster general and so was a further step to the displacement of British authority. When on July 21, the Congress resolved to open the ports of the colonies to free trade with all nations other than those falling under the nonimportation ban, it thereby assumed the prerogatives of a government over commercial policy, and not only supplanted Parliament in this process but appeared to preempt the liberties of individual colonies. In this measure the Congress had moved too far ahead of opinion among its constituencies; colonies, as they became independent, assumed the power to make their own customs regulations and to determine the elements of their own general economic policies.

## Prospects for Reconciliation

In its rejection of Lord North's olive branch, Congress stood on ground that Americans had occupied in principle though with varying degrees of completeness ever since the Stamp Act. The reply stated that Parliament could not decide whether or for what purposes colonial assemblies should raise money by taxation or how such money was to be spent; Congress went further and rejected any right claimed by Parliament "to intermeddle with provisions for the support of civil government," denounced the record of parliamentary abuses, and scornfully declared that this proposition was held up to the world to deceive it into the belief that the only matter in dispute was the mere method of levying taxes.

Hopes for reconciliation rested partly on the belief that the king, and his ministers, and members of Parliament, could be convinced of their errors; but they also drew support from the theory that neither the ministry nor Parliament was truly in touch with the people. The Americans therefore needed to persuade the people of Britain to unite with them against their own representatives. This made it necessary to address the people with their reasons for rejecting the conciliatory proposition, which was done along with Dickinson's petition to the king. The address declared that the colonists could not enter into free discussions with a bayonet at their breast, told the British of the cruelties already inflicted, and argued again that ministers could not spend the money raised by colonial assemblies. The Americans would not grasp the shadow and give up the substance.

Congress faced an enemy in arms, and needed peace on its frontiers. The Americans had never appealed to their Indian neighbors with greater concern for their welfare; a message to the Six Nations explained the trouble between the colonists and their unkind father and asked for peace and understanding. Meanwhile three Indian departments were established and commissioners of Indian affairs were appointed. A close watch was kept continually on Indian relationships and developments.

Before adjourning for a recess, Congress intervened to try to quiet the menacing dispute between settlers from Pennsylvania and Connecticut in the Wyoming Valley, a rivalry that was to vex congressional counsels for many months and show little sign of yielding to pleas for self-restraint. An executive committee was given power to act for the Congress during the recess.

By these acts, almost a year before it took the plunge into independence, Congress had effectively committed itself to positions from which it would have been impossible to retreat without coercion. Yet moderate men could still believe that grounds for reconciliation not only existed but had even improved. Thomas Johnson, later governor of Maryland, and now a delegate, reviewed the position to Horatio Gates during the recess. His analysis of American strategy justified the petition to the king. They wished, first to establish their liberties, and secondly to achieve reunion with Great Britain. If the petition was granted, the feelings of 1763 would be restored; but Johnson believed Britain would be ruined by the delay if the petition were not granted, but were so far attended to as to lay the groundwork for negotiation. Meanwhile, the colonies needed to keep in touch with a strong party headed by Chatham and other old Whigs in British politics; Johnson here fell into the conventional self-laid American trap of following some of the most outworn opposition rhetoric in Britain by blaming the influence of the Scotsmen, Bute and Mansfield. Bute had lost all influence in or soon after 1763; Mansfield did not determine administration policy, though his conservative views were in keeping with the majority. Johnson's criticism also mentioned Lord North; but he omitted the king. He and the influential school of middle colony moderates, who still had the power to hold the Congress back from precipitate measures, could base some of their infirm hopes on the notion that the king was the victim of evil counsellors. This was perhaps the last American illusion to die.

When the Congress reconvened, the nonexportation agreement, timed for September 10, had officially begun to operate. The delegates of many exporting interests urged the unwisdom of the policy. Their reasons may have been self-interested, but their reasoning carried some conviction, for they could argue that America must export in order to buy its war supplies abroad. Robert R. Livingston of New York put his finger on a delicate point when he warned members that "the people will feel, and will say, that Congress tax them and oppress them worse than Parliament[8]." But the majority held to the clear and simple need for a conspicuously uniform policy, and they concluded by confirming the Association. The question of whether to order the arrest of Lord Dunmore, who was levying war in Virginia, caused a sharp discussion which again brought forward the fear of independence. Johnson, still speaking for nonprovocation, admitted that he saw less and less prospect of reconciliation every day; but he would not render it impossible. He backed his plea for moderate policies in Congress with a warning that four colonies, North Carolina, Virginia, Pennsylvania, and New York had strong parties in them who were still willing to make peace through concessions "inconsistent with the rights of America." He did not want to give them an opportunity to withdraw from the common front so far formed. Five or six weeks more, he thought, would give the final determination of the people of Great Britain. In a similar vein, when Richard Henry Lee moved to put a stop to the "ministerial" posts—that is, the running of the postal service under British auspices—he met the same kind of opposition.[9] Thomas Willing, the great Philadelphia merchant, regarded the measure as offensive and improper at the time; it might impair the prospects of negotiation.

These hesitations could not impede the Congress from following the courses it had already marked out. One of the first tasks after the recess was to improve its working efficiency. The delegates who left records of their time in Philadelphia were clearly under very heavy and sustained pressure. Silas Deane told his wife that he rose at five and was writing to her at midnight; the session began at nine and continued until three or four; committees filled many other periods. Philadelphia society also offered a number of generous dinners, whose splendor and variety astonished John Adams and caused trepidation to his Puritan scruples. No doubt, different delegates took their duties and pleasures in different ways. Those at the center of events had probably less time than they really needed to read and reflect; before the end of the year John Adams had sought leave to return home from sheer exhaustion. The looseness of rules of procedure also protracted discussions. Many members were fond of the sound of their own voices, and discoursed at length on matters that required action. At times it must have seemed to the more ardent spirits that if the variety of opinions and the self-indulgence of speakers were not brought under some tighter discipline they would make coherent policy or decisive action impossible (see Document 3-c).

The most practical answer to these difficulties lay in the appointment of committees. On September 18, 1775, it was agreed to set up a secret committee to purchase military supplies. This Secret Committee, as it was soon called, was responsible for dealing with commerce. But conferring great powers on small bodies of men produced its own resentments; the Secret Committee made an agreement with Robert Morris, Willing's partner, for the purchase of gunpowder, on terms that gave Morris a very safe profit. The debate that followed the revelation of these terms in full Congress was acrimonious. But Robert Morris soon joined the Congress as a delegate from Pennsylvania, and his mastery of business established him as a man of great influence over future economic policy. John Adams was shocked by the numerous evidences of personal favors and concessions to regional interests that he constantly saw in the conduct of business; he began to wonder whether America's morals would stand the strain that lay ahead.

During October, the Congress debated naval problems. They faced the might of the world's greatest sea power; in the long run, as would soon be seen, they would need a French alliance; but at least there was a use for vessels that could intercept troop movements in limited actions, and John Adams felt proud of his contribution to the creation of the force that was to become the United States Navy. The Secret Committee of Correspondence, set up in November, evolved into a foreign policy committee, and with the earlier Secret Committee on Commerce, functioned as the center for long-term policy (see Document 4). It was not until 1777 that a formal foreign Affairs Committee was created. The members of these crucial committees were elected by ballot, and membership gave an indication of the caution with which the Congress as a whole continued to move. John Jay, whose influence was not unconnected with his conservatism, came to John Adams at one point during the winter to explain to him why he had been omitted from both the secret committees. His exclusion was due to his close connections with Samuel Adams and Richard Henry Lee, who were viewed with great suspicion. Adams rather self-revealingly disclaimed any ambition to be considered the "first man in the Congress" but admitted his surprise that no delegate from Massachusetts had been given a place on either committee. He declined, however, to buy himself a place by dropping his intimacy with his cousin or Lee. He added a word of his suspicions about the entrepeneurial motives operating in the Committee on Commerce, but told Jay that the great division was on independence and the mode of carrying on the war.

## Increased Colonial Autonomy:  British Retaliation

Conservatives could not halt the pace of events outside, however. In June the Congress had given the people of Massachusetts the assurance that they owed no allegiance to royal officers whose actions were contrary to the charter, and advised them on procedures for electing representatives to a provincial assembly; in November it answered calls for advice from New Hampshire and South Carolina with instructions for establishing what was to all intents and purposes an independent government. Plans were now going forward for a military advance into Canada. The basic strategic thinking, which anticipated a dangerous British advance from Canadian bases, was probably sound, but the truth was that the American armies were neither supplied nor trained for the exigencies of such an expedition. These movements were not intended to rule out further negotiation, however. The king had issued a new proclamation on August 23 denouncing the American rebellion; Congress replied on December 6, with yet another statement of its position. Rebellion was disclaimed; nor did the Congress admit the charge that its acts were unlawful. It did state a view of the constitution at which only a few thinkers had firmly arrived during the preceding year. In affirming allegiance to the king, the Congress now repudiated all allegiance to Parliament.

These bold steps opened the way to new hopes or fearful dangers, depending on the viewer's ultimate aspirations. They corresponded to the needs which the Congress existed to defend; but they also tended to promote those needs into a virtual requirement of colonial autonomy. The conservatives in the Congress had been left behind for the time being, but they were neither isolated nor unrepresentative. Their hesitation about irreversible commitments and fears about where they were being led reflected much public sentiment, which was strongly represented in the legislatures of the proprietary colonies and New York. When these assemblies read the signposts marked "Independence," they quickly acted to obstruct the road. On November 9, the Pennsylvania assembly gave stiff instructions to its new delegation to the Continental Congress: "We strictly enjoin you, that you, in behalf of this colony, dissent from and utterly reject any propositions, should such be made, that may cause or lead to a separation from our mother country, or a change in the form of this government."[10] The latter point alluded to the risks of internal instability, and soon proved to be well founded. Although this resolution drew attacks from the press, its tenor was reflected by similar instructions in New Jersey, Delaware, Maryland, and New York before the end of the year.

Two of America's younger spokesmen, the immigrant Scottish lawyer James Wilson of Pennsylvania, and Thomas Jefferson of Virginia had announced in pamphlets in 1774 the seemingly paradoxical view that the colonies owed allegiance to the king while holding themselves entirely independent of Parliament. Wilson had in fact reached this conclusion in 1770, but had withheld it from publication when the dispute seemed to simmer down. The paradox arose from the fact that Parliament itself was constitutionally incomplete without the presence of the king. The full sovereign power of Great Britain was exercized by the king-in-Parliament. The colonial claim now was that the king's relationship to each colonial assembly was precisely the same as his relationship to the Parliament of Westminster. This ingenious argument, which might in theory have formed a new basis for the relationship, was easier to believe from the American than the British side of the water. To most British minds it appeared merely absurd. One needed only an elementary grasp of constitutional law to know that there could be no empire without sovereignty and no sovereignty without Parliament. It was doubtful whether any of America's friends in Parliament could really come to terms with the new American view of the constitution. The opposing positions were theoretically irreconcilable—at least in the eighteenth century—and clarification would only serve to define the difference rather than to bring hope of reconciliation.

Before the end of the year bad news began to arrive from the Canadian quarter. Richard Smith of New Jersey noted in his diary that General Arnold, whose force was near Quebec, had not enough men to surround the city and only enough powder for five rounds apiece; General Richard Montgomery's soldiers were very disobedient, and many of them had gone home without leave. Washington was also suffering a great shortage of powder; it was reported that desertions among his Connecticut troops were depleting his army. As a matter of fact, Washington had quickly developed a very low opinion of the New England troops under his command, which tended to correspond with and thereby to confirm the prejudices of a southern landlord as to the quality of a medley of New England farmers. Under winter conditions the news moved slowly from the North, but worse was to follow. Before the actions were over and the colonial forces withdrawn, Montgomery was dead and Arnold wounded and temporarily out of action. But Congress was spared this news until the middle of January.

Meanwhile, Lord North took further steps to assist the colonists to make up their minds. In December he secured the passage of the American Prohibitory Act, which began by repealing the Boston Port Act and the two restraining laws dating from the spring of 1775. His new measure was more comprehensive. It would bring colonial commerce to an end until they had given their submission to British commissioners who were to be appointed for the purpose; all American vessels and their cargoes could now be seized as if they belonged to an enemy at war; as was customary in naval warfare, the naval commanders and sailors making the seizures were allowed to treat the goods as lawful prizes. When conducted without cover of law, this highly remunerative application of the system of individual incentive was known as piracy.

Opposition speakers rightly called the bill a declaration of war. Fox, who understood that it would bind the colonies together under the leadership of their separatists, remarked sardonically that it should have been entitled, "a Bill for more effectually carrying into execution the resolves of the Congress." Sea passages were slow in mid-winter, however, and it was not until the middle of February that delegates to the American Congress received the news of this act. In the interval, American public opinion was prepared by more blows struck closer to home.

## Notes

1. For information on British politics, see Bernard Donoughue, *British Politics and the American Revolution* (London: Macmillan & Co., 1964).

2. For an excellent account of the interplay between British politics and the views that shaped colonial policies, see Pauline Maier, *From Resistance to Revolution* (New York: Alfred Knopf, 1972).

3. Edmund Burke, *Speeches on the American War, etc.*, ed. George A. Billias (Boston, The Gregg Press, 1972), p. 101.

4. C. E. Carter, ed., *The Correspondence of General Thomas Gage, 1763-1775*, 2 vols. (New Haven: Yale University Press, 1933), vol. 2, pp. 658-59.

5. Edmund C. Burnett, ed., *Letters of Members of the Continental Congress* (Washington, D.C.: The Carnegie Institution, 1921), vol. 1, p. 259.

6. Ibid., p. 349.

7. Ibid., p. 176.

8. L. H. Butterfield et al., eds., *The Diary of John Adams* (Cambridge: Harvard University Press, 1921), vol. 2, p. 189.

9. Ibid., p. 200.

10. Peter Force, *American Archives* (Washington: 1837-53) Fourth ser., vol. 3, pp. 1792-3; Merrill Jensen, *The Founding of a Nation* (New York: Oxford Univ. Press, 1968), p. 641.

# 4

## The Quickening of Independence

### Persuading "Unconvinced Americans"

The surviving records disclose very little of the inner character of Congress during this critical winter and spring of 1775-1776. Much that took place on the floor of the hall was influenced, even decided, in private meetings elsewhere. When Jay told John Adams that he could have seats on the secret committees if he would abandon his deeply disliked intimacy with his cousin and Richard Henry Lee, he offered one of the most revealing clues to the problem of this inner structure. The hostility was directed against a caucus of activists who met frequently to discuss forthcoming business and concert tactics. It was not John Adams, but Samuel, who was at the center of these clandestine maneuvers. The caucus also included Richard Henry Lee, George Wythe of Virginia, and probably others, but it is not clear that John regularly attended their meetings. The active genius was Sam, who was now practicing in Philadelphia his extraordinary flair for that kind of political management and manipulation which, by seizing illegitimate ground and holding it against counterattack, succeeds in changing the definition of legitimacy. Conservatives feared and hated him; and many others must have regarded him with the most intense suspicion—to which his exclusion from committees bore witness. But the caucus exerted increasing influence on the conduct of business as events called for new policies. It decided who should speak and with what arguments in the course of debates; it foresaw and provided for contingencies; whether its work decided the outcome, or merely corresponded with the tune of events, its aims were clear—to conservative eyes, diabolically clear. Samuel Adams was also ceaselessly active outside Congress, sowing information, rallying opinion, quietly menacing the conservatives. His tireless and shrewd activity left few traces compared to the numerous letters and writings of his cousin, but his work was probably more effective. And yet Samuel Adams appreciated the limits within which he and his associates were free to operate. "We cannot make events. Our business is wisely to improve them," he is said to have once remarked.[1] All their activity would have been useless if forces outside their control had moved in different ways; and until the doors of reconciliation were shut in the faces of the most patient Anglophiles, both the Adamses made themselves and their colony very unpopular. Moderate men tended to recoil from them and seek the shelter of lingering conservative hopes of reconciliation. The strength and persistence of these hopes and the staying power of conciliationist influence in the persons of Dickinson, Jay, Livingston, Edward Rutledge and, more surprisingly, of James Wilson, remains at least as impressive as the power of the slowly accumulating argument for separation.

The Congress began the new year facing two urgent needs at home, both of them arising from dissidence and doubt. One was to convince the doubters; the other was to coerce the dissidents. On January 2, it adopted a resolution intended to persuade "unconvinced Americans." Provincial conventions and assemblies were recommended to publish and distribute as widely as possible the proceedings of this and former congresses, as well as the speeches made in both Houses of Parliament by English patriots sympathizing with American grievances, and such other pamphlets and papers "as tend to elucidate the American cause." It was important that British authority could be cited in favor of America. The resolution looked on doubting Americans as persons whose errors were produced from want of information rather than from want of virtue or public spirit. But coercion followed. Measures were to be taken to disarm Americans who were enemies to the cause.

The coercive arm was soon brought to bear against those inhabitants of Queen's County, New York, who had voted against sending delegates to the Provincial Congress, and similar steps were soon taken in Tryon County. The truth was that the widespread and outspoken dissidence in New York was a source of grave anxiety; it gave every encouragement to the British forces and undermined the confidence of such other Americans as might be inclined to doubt. It was a comfort to be able to announce on February 8, that former restrictions imposed on the inhabitants of Richmond County were to be lifted as they had freely elected delegates to their Provincial Congress.

When the Congress took upon itself to issue bills, it incurred the obligation to make their credit good. But already people were refusing to accept them. Where faith failed, the Congress, assuming one of the virtual prerogatives of sovereignty, again resorted to coercive measures to sustain its currency. On January 11, it ordered that persons refusing to accept congressional bills were to be tried by their city, county, or district committee and if convicted were to be treated as enemies and precluded from all trade and intercourse with the inhabitants of the colonies. This resolution allowed for appeals to the assembly or convention; in each colony, therefore, either the assembly acting in a revolutionary capacity, or a specifically revolutionary body, was now told to act as a court of appeal. Increasingly the powers and prerogatives of government were passing into the hands of revolutionary bodies.

In the same month the independence-minded members of the Congress received a new injection of outside assistance. Thomas Paine, an East Anglian corset maker who had worked formerly as an English customs officer, but had lost his job on publishing a protest against the low pay of his profession, had arrived only two years earlier in Philadelphia. He was getting to know the political dissidents and radicals in the city and developed a rapid, instinctive sympathy with the American cause. In January, 1776, he published an anonymous pamphlet under the blunt title, *Common Sense*. The title had been suggested by Franklin, whom many people thought responsible for the whole work. But it was very much Paine's own in thought and style. Paine used a mixture of somewhat artificial imagery ("The palaces of kings are built on the ruins of the bowers of paradise") and blunt speech (George III was "the royal brute of Great Britain") to tell people things that many of them already knew, or thought, but hesitated to admit. That was his power. He believed himself to be far more original a thinker than he really was, but he did break sharply with lingering traditions of allegiance and loyalty. The thrust of Paine's argument against the British connection derived its strength from his violent attack on inherited power. With a show of respect for biblical authority, he contrasted the equality of man in his original state with the spurious authority of kings. The implications reached not only across the Atlantic but deep into the principles on which American colonial institutions were constructed. John Adams, who believed it would be dangerous to interfere with the existing suffrage restrictions, saw the drift of Paine's argument and did not like what he saw. It tended to disturb respect for authority not only abroad, but in America. Moreover, Adams somewhat resented the fame that the pamphlet was gathering; he had been putting these arguments to Congress for the previous year, and had gained small praise for his efforts. When he learned the author's identify, he spent an evening with him, in which their differences soon became clearer than their affinities; Paine compounded his offenses by irreverent comments on the Bible, for which Adams called him to task.

Adams might complain privately that Paine had added nothing to the previous year's arguments in Congress; but the difference was that Congress was still meeting in secret. Paine's pamphlet ran through twenty-five printings within the next few months, compared with one printing of Jefferson's *Summary View* and of Wilson's learned treatise on the *Legislative Authority of Parliament*. Estimates suggest that *Common Sense* sold some 120,000 copies.[2] Of course the effects were not immediate. Copies had to be carried by wagon from Philadelphia, and comments show that it was still making an initial impact in March. But that impact was being felt while other events drove in the same direction. A worried New York Tory wrote on March 22: "There is a great talk of independence, and the unthinking multitude are mad for it ... A pamphlet called Common Sense, has carried off its thousands; an answer thereto is come out, but instantly seized from the printer's shop, and burnt in the street, as unfit to be read at this time."[3]

## The Need for a French Alliance

About the middle of February, the tide in Congress began to move definitively toward independence. Delegates gained new confidence that if they moved that way their constituents would support them. The earlier acts of the Congress had obviously pointed along a course that would be increasingly hard to retract; *Common Sense* helped to free people's thoughts, letting them discuss what had formerly been suppressed. But so did the objective facts to which all had some degree of access. Every action of the local committees rested on an assertion of revolutionary as opposed to royal authority; each time a revolutionary body acted in defense of its existing position it helped to make independence more logical than any other solution. From the Tory or moderate points of view the tragedy was that nothing concrete actually happened to arrest this hastening tide or to offer an alternative course. Moderates had virtually to invent or imagine alternatives and spin out their hopes with gossip about negotiations.

They continued to resist the trend, and to treat every issue as raising alternative possibilities. John Adams kept muttering that debates were protracted, irrelevant issues drawn out to excessive lengths, to avoid decisions; but all the time the moderate alternatives grew less and less plausible (see Document 5). In February, Congress debated an alliance with France. It was clear by now that if the Americans were to maintain a war effort they would need supplies beyond their own productive powers. "The consequence of making alliances" remarked John Penn of North Carolina, whose ruminations show him to have been anxious for reconciliation at this date (February 14) "is perhaps total separation with Britain and without something of that sort we may not be able to provide what is necessary for our defense." He added that he was sending "a pamphlet called Common Sense published here about a month ago."[4] John Adams, commenting on the same debate, recognized France's need in her own national interests to see North America independent of Great Britain. This debate was probably stimulated by the fact that, early in February, certain colonists on opposite sides of the question of independence began to discuss a new threat to the future of British America. They believed in their own importance to Britain, and this confidence made it possible to believe that Britain would go to extreme lengths to bring the colonies back into a state of subordination—even to the length of agreeing to partition the continent with France, and perhaps with Spain. The first prominent reply to Paine's *Common Sense* raised this danger and warned Americans of the risks they ran. Charles Inglis's pamphlet, *The True Interest of America Impartially Stated, in Certain Strictures Upon a Pamphlet Intitled Common Sense* (Philadelphia, 1776) stated that France and Spain had made an offer of assistance to Britain in the contest with the colonies. The idea seems to have arisen first as a result of a visit to Versailles by Lord Mansfield in the late summer of 1774; but as it was now 1776 and nothing further had been heard, the threat can hardly have seemed very formidable. There is a possibility that it was renewed by the British government, not as a serious proposition, but solely to frighten the Americans. In the autumn of 1775 a Frenchman called Roubaud, acting as amanuensis to John Pownall, undersecretary at the American department in London, fabricated a scheme on these lines and tried to interest Vergennes, the French chief minister. Vergennes saw through the subterfuge and dismissed it. But the British admiralty may have caught wind of it and transmitted the idea for reception in America. In any event, influential colonists did start to discuss the possibility in February, and continued to worry about it for several months, even after independence had been declared—since it might still be used to tempt the French into an anti-American association with Britain. Colonists also took anxious note of the arrival of French troops in the French West Indies, which would be consistent with plans for renewed ventures on the continent.[5]

These possibilities made the matter of a French alliance more urgent. On March 1, the Secret Committee (the one dating from September 1775) instructed Silas Deane of Connecticut to go to France and begin to make purchases, providing 200,000 dollars for the purpose. The Committee of Secret Correspondence (which afterwards became the Committee for Foreign Affairs) also gave Deane instructions, which included sounding the Comte de Vergennes as to France's attitude in case of "a total separation from Great Britain," which was treated as probable. He was to let the French know that American commerce was likely to go to France rather than to Great Britain. America needed clothing and arms for twenty-five thousand men, as well as ammunition and field guns. Vergennes was to be given to understand that in the event of independence the Americans would be interested in an alliance.

The American fear of partition was understandable, considering the recent partition of Poland by Austria, Russia, and Prussia, and the also recent suppression of a national rising in Corsica, which was much on people's minds. But if the British did use it in the hope of disciplining the Americans, it worked the wrong way. It was just as reasonable to argue that the threat made agreement with France more necessary and that independence was America's only safeguard, for without the declared intent of independence, France would obviously not be interested in an alliance. Each side in the colonial debate used the partition threat as an additional reason for following its own policy. But insofar as it stimulated the move toward France, it can be said to have contributed to the advance of American independence.

These forward looking measures failed to satisfy John Adams. He felt that he lacked adequate support even from his Massachusetts colleagues. Dickinson meanwhile had drawn up a new petition, from which people still hoped for relief.

Another step towards sovereignty was the decision on February 17 to open American ports to the rest of the world (not including Britain or Ireland); the reasons were to be published in Europe and the West Indies. Then, apparently about February 19, the news of Lord North's American Prohibitory Act reached Philadelphia. On that date Oliver Wolcott reported the news, adding that a British commission was to follow, which firm Whigs considered as an insidious maneuver. The act actually provided for the appointment of commissioners whose duty would apparently be confined to accepting the submission of the Americans; yet for two or three months after this, rumors of British commissioners kept circulating, repeatedly reviving moderate hopes of a negotiation. The terms of the act treated the Americans as enemies and could only serve to harden their resistance; yet the news from Britain made matters still more complicated for American moderates, for they were also given to understand that the Rockingham Whigs would abandon them if they aimed at independence, but would stand by them if not. With these reports the Americans also heard firm news of foreign regiments being raised to make war on them.

For those not already committed to independence the prospects were now intensely discouraging. And many of those who were committed might have preferred to find some alternative to the prolonged horrors and miseries of the war that was to follow. Both Tories and moderate patriots knew and warned their fellow Americans that the conflict on which they were embarking was a civil war. British Americans would fight their English kin; Americans would fight each other. Yet the spring brought other news from New England. After a prolonged siege, General Howe accepted Washington's terms for evacuation of Boston: the city was to be spared, and Howe would be allowed to leave by sea, taking with him those American Loyalists who preferred the refuge of Canada or Great Britain. The whole operation, slowed down by the fear of smallpox in the town, was completed by March 22, when hordes of happy Americans flocked into the damaged but liberated city that had so long symbolized their liberties. This news gave immense encouragement to Americans getting ready to resist elsewhere.

Congress was now turning much of its attention to the economic implications of a fight that would close America's chief source of overseas supplies so long as it lasted. Plans were developed and announced in the form of a congressional resolution for economic development and the improvement of agriculture. On April 1, it was decided to establish a treasury—another indispensable office of government. Differences had been brewing for many months about the disposal of the stored tea, imported before the ban went into force, but prohibited from reaching the market. Not until April 13 did Congress at last agree to allow the merchants to sell the tea in their stores. Some delegates thought the profits should accrue to the community rather than to the merchants; this view did not prevail, but the resolution releasing the tea did lay down a scale of prices. Then, a fortnight later, the Congress gave way to market forces and decided to relax price regulation. A decision also made in April, to order that Governor Eden of Maryland and all his papers be seized, gave rise to visible anxiety; there were still those who held it to be unwisely provocative. But the evidence of Eden's hostility was enough for the majority.

By the early days of May, when delegates began to make formal moves toward independence, Congress in these ways already exercized many of the prerogatives of a government. In certain respects it made wider claims than were later conferred by the Articles of Confederation, which had no powers over colonial ports and no authority over prices. It was already beginning to be true that some Americans were feeling the arm of Congress, and of the Continental army, more heavily than they had felt the remote powers of

British government. As Congress became progressively more committed, some of the heady enthusiasm of earlier months showed marked signs of ebbing. Washington found it particularly difficult to induce New Englanders to serve in the Continental army, a reluctance which can be understood in the light of the low pay of private soldiers, the enormous differences in social rank assumed by the officers, and the floggings which Washington regarded as normal means of enforcing discipline. The capture of Boston relaxed these immediate tensions and freed Washington to bring his army south. It also spurred enthusiasm in the hesitant ranks of New York.

## Remaining Conservative Obstacles

While events narrowed the choices of moderate men, those who were already committed either to action or to restraint were appalled at the difficulties caused by the passions, or the block-headedness, of their opponents. "The middle way is none at all" John Adams told Horatio Gates before the end of March. What then was the problem? It lay in the fear of openly avowing independence. "Independency is a Hobgoblin of so frightful Mien, that it would throw a delicate Person into Fits to look it in the Face."[6] The most serious obstacles in Congress itself still had their sources in the provinces where conservative elements held the strongest grip on the assemblies or conventions—New York and the proprietary provinces of Pennsylvania and Maryland.

Lack of enthusiasm for the Whig cause was nothing new in New York. As late as November, 1775, the Second Provincial Congress collapsed for want of a quorum. The timid hesitation of the Whigs and the resentful determination of the Tories held the province back from positive action. The difficulties of the Whigs were compounded by dangers both external and internal. The external problem lay in New York Harbor, where British men-of-war were at anchor, and gave the traders a brisk business in supplying the wants of the sailors; but these same ships could too easily position themselves to bombard the city. These dangers forced many obviously reluctant partisans to take sides. About one-third of the 104 members of the New York Chamber of Commerce remained loyal to the crown, while another third was neutral. The Whig leadership had fallen by this time to the Livingston connection, but the family itself was disunited, and their party was deeply conservative and almost as anxious to avert a popular revolution as to throw off British oppression. With the traditional leadership in splinters, the Livingstonian Whigs were increasingly vulnerable to the hammering of the city mechanics (the common name for skilled artisans), who spent the winter and spring of 1776 insisting on stronger representation in the Provincial Convention. If New York steered towards its own form of government, conservative Whigs could plainly foresee that the power to control the political future of the province might slip from their grasp. In Carl Becker's famous phrase, the struggle over home rule became a struggle over who should rule at home.

The Second Provincial Congress did not prove a source of much strength to the movement for independence in New York. It competed with the official assembly, in which the Whigs won an overwhelming majority in elections held in mid-February. But a Whig victory in New York rebuked the Tories without elevating the Radicals, and the leadership remained much as before. While James Duane, a genuine reconciliationist, held out hopes from the prospect of British commissioners, such conservative Whigs as Jay and R. R. Livingston were now moving perceptibly towards independence. "Another year of war and devastation will confirm me a republican," Livingston admitted at the time of the assembly elections.[7] Jay went so far as to advocate that the Provincial Congress levy taxes, which would constitute an assertion of governmental power; no American could doubt that taxation was linked with representation through constitutional forms which implied consent to being governed by the power that laid and collected taxes. Before the end of March, the Provincial Convention complied, though not on its own initiative, with the Continental Congress's instructions to disarm the Tories. In the middle of April the New York Committee of Safety was told by General Washington that New Yorkers must stop trading with the British warships, and this order was also obeyed. Elections to a Third Provincial Congress held in April produced results that must have disappointed the radicals, but remained somewhat difficult to interpret.

All fourteen counties now voted to send delegates, a great improvement on former records. But the members were in many cases not the men the radicals wished to see in the convention. The choices before New Yorkers were closing down; but voters still preferred not to force the pace of events. By the end of April, however, there was evidence of a growing consensus which at least seemed to exclude Tory solutions; the New York press in previous months had carried a great variety of correspondence, but now the advocates of loyalty to Britain fell silent. With the British fleet in the harbor, and with British and American armies threatening the city, it was difficult for New Yorkers to think through their problems on the basis of abstract principles. Mistakes of judgment might have devastating consequences. Throughout May and June the Third Provincial Congress parried with increasing demands for a commitment from their own mechanics and from their delegates in Philadelphia. Before dissolving, the Third Provincial Congress handed on to its successor the responsibility for subscribing to the Declaration of Independence, which had already been promulgated in Philadelphia. Beyond that event, however, the British occupation of New York City, which became their headquarters throughout the war, distorted the politics of the new state and deprived the well-organized city mechanics of an influence they might otherwise have gained.

## Pennsylvania Votes for Independence: Defeat for the Moderates

Radicals of the lower economic classes took an equally forceful but far more successful part in remaking the politics of Pennsylvania. Until the radicals broke into city politics in the early months of 1776, the Philadelphia Committee of Inspection and Observation was in the safe control of the customary custodians of public affairs; like other public bodies, it was composed of gentry and wealthy merchants. The radicals upset this equilibrium in new elections in February and then outflanked the Pennsylvania Assembly by calling for a Provincial Convention. This call followed a refusal by the assembly to alter its instructions to the Pennsylvania delegates to the Continental Congress so as to permit them to vote for independence. Continental and provincial politics were now tightly interlocked. Radicals in Pennsylvania had complained about the under-representation of the country and western districts, a state of affairs which the assembly had steadily refused to reform over several years. Now, under heavy pressure, and with the imperial crisis shaking their control, the assembly agreed to add seventeen seats to its own numbers. This decision which was taken early in March, opened new prospects for the next assembly elections on May 1.

The campaigns reflected traditional social divisions, now coming under stress from radical assertions of equality of status. Yet the politics of deference, mixed with uncertainties about the future, continued to exert a considerable hold on the voters. The Philadelphia moderates did not stand as extreme conservatives, and recognized that their hands might be forced. They promised to seek "peace on honorable terms" but they added that, "If the fatal necessity should evidently arise, which will justify new declarations, and a change of measures, *such men* will never dissent from the general views of their constituents." The results gave the moderates a narrow victory.

The politics of the Continental Congress and those of the host city had always been maintained in a somewhat tense proximity. Galloway, as we have seen, believed that Sam Adams used the mob, or threats of it, to intimidate delegates—and Galloway was certainly a victim of such attempts. Adams was now intensely active in the lodging houses and social meeting places of delegates and in the conclaves of the Philadelphia radicals. With his tactile feeling for the emotions which lay just below the surface of political actuality, held in check by the caution of prudent leadership, he remarked on April 30 that a battle would arouse the people more effectively than any other event. The reports of the British burning of the Massachusetts port of Falmouth in Massachusetts and of Norfolk in Virginia did a great deal of good from Adams's point of view. They convinced doubting people that the British were their irreconcilable enemies. Such acts were intended to strike terror and produce opposite results, and on May 6, such effects came unpleasantly close to home. Two British warships passed up the Schuylkill, shelling Pennsylvania settlements and causing a violent scare in the capital. This was not what Sam Adams meant by a battle. It may well have contributed to the continued holding out for some other form of settlement. Dickinson's long-lived moderation exasperated the Adamses and men like Richard Henry Lee, but it continued to reflect much of the solid sentiment of Philadelphia.

The people of Pennsylvania had taken a long time to develop any warmth for their suffering comrades in Boston. The Quaker city, by no means having outlived the powerful influence of that quiet but active sect, could still recall that Boston had actually hanged Quakers in the previous century; the merchants of the two cities had distrusted each other in the more recent nonimportation movements. As to their own interests, the fact was that the politics of the backcountry were by no means clearly reflected in the capital or centrally involved with the imperial crisis, and moreover that several years of economic stability and reasonable comfort had left many Philadelphians with the feeling that they had more to lose than to gain from an upheaval. The Pennsylvania radicals had failed to gain control of their own assembly, which moderate opponents of independence still dominated. The Continental Congress, checked in its own freedom of action by this resistance, now came to the aid of its neighbors. On May 10, acting on an earlier motion introduced by John Adams, it was resolved to recommend the assemblies and conventions of the United Colonies, "where no government sufficient to the exigencies of their affairs have hitherto been established, to adopt such governments as shall, in the opinion of the representatives of the people, best conduce to the happiness and safety of their constituents in particular, and of America in general". This momentous decision was thought to require a preamble before being introduced to the people, and a small committee, consisting of John Adams, Edward Rutledge, and Richard Henry Lee, was appointed to prepare the draft.

The Philadelphia radicals seized the opportunity presented by this congressional initiative. They convened a public meeting, which brought some four thousand people together to press the assembly with a demand for a government based on the "authority of the people." But the moderates were not played out yet. Dickinson had not opposed Adams's resolution because he was able to maintain that it did not apply to Pennsylvania, which already possessed a perfectly adequate charter. The Radicals replied that the charter was a gift of the crown; what they demanded was the substitution of the people as the source of authority. On May 21, the moderates drew up their reply, a formal Remonstrance setting out the charter as the rightful basis of Pennsylvania government. The problem for both sides was now to get the country districts to take a firm stand, but as moderate emissaries carried the Remonstrance into the country, they encountered violent resistance. By the middle of May, the Philadelphia Committee of Correspondence under James Cannon had already established contacts with every county and township in Pennsylvania; local committees, warned of the coming struggle for the loyalty of the backcountry, organized violent resistance which drove the remonstrants out of their communities. Whether they represented actual majorities will always be impossible to say. They possessed the initiative, the organization and the capacity for mobilizing and inflaming opinion in the way that invariably leaves the less committed individuals behind, and outflanks and destroys the actual opposition.

Dickinson's hopes of saving the assembly were killed on May 27, when news arrived that the Virginia Provincial Convention had instructed its delegates in Congress to vote for independence. The independents who had seats in the assembly boycotted its meeting on June 1, and agreed to return only on the condition that the moderates would debate a change in the instructions to the province's delegates in the Continental Congress. Yet even when new instructions appeared, they were indecisive. The radical solution to the problem of procedure was a simple one; they had it in their power by absenting themselves to cause the assembly's collapse. It met for the last time on June 14. Pennsylvania at last followed other colonies which had set conventions in place of assemblies, but even as it did so, independent ranks began to show signs of splitting over the new constitution in which their more radical members now clearly aimed to lay the basis for radical power in the new state.

Charles Thomson, the Philadelphia radical whose influence had helped to form the secret lines of connection from the city to the Congress, was somewhat dismayed by the quality of the membership sent up by the county committees; many of the new men, he commented, were "wholly unequal" to the affairs of the state. The body to which these unlikely delegates had been elected was called a Provincial Conference, deputed to lay down the rules for a convention. When that convention met, it was virtually a creation of the committees of correspondence and the radical forces that had been assuming power throughout the colony and had brought about the downfall of the assembly. No moderate or conservative base remained. Pennsylvania's vote for independence was no longer in doubt.

## Notes

1. John C. Miller, *Samuel Adams, Pioneer in Propaganda* (Boston: Little, Brown & Co., 1936), p. 342. Miller's footnote, however, only cites a letter *to* Adams, not by him. The remark is not very characteristic.

2. For the publishing history of pamphlets in this period, see Thomas B. Adams, *American Independence* (Providence, R. I.: Broon U. P., 1965).

3. Bernard Mason, *The Road to Independence* (Lexington, Ky.: University of Kentucky Press, 1966), p. 162.

4. Edmund C. Burnett, ed., *Letters of Members of the Continental Congress* (Washington, D.C.: The Carnegie Institution, 1921), vol. 1, p. 349.

5. For this view and the information about Roubaud and the American discussion of the threat of partition, see James H. Hutson, "The Partition Treaty and the Declaration of American Independence," *Journal of American History* 58, no. 4 (March, 1972).

6. Burnett, *Letters*, vol. 1, p. 405-6.

7. Mason, *The Road to Independence*, p. 140.

# 5

# Independence Declared

## The Options Close

After the Congress had recommended the colonies to establish independent governments, the period of some seven weeks until the actual decision for American independence seems in retrospect to have been inordinately long. The delay was due not so much to distances and difficulties of communication as to the continuation of the interplay between the undecided colonial conventions and the now more militant spirit of Congress. It was due also, though perhaps to a lesser degree, to the survival of moderate sentiments in Congress itself. The resolution of May 10 stood for several days without formal promulgation while John Adams drafted a preamble. When that was done, and the action was ready to be justified to the colonies, the formal adoption followed on the fifteenth.

John Adams was exultant. "This day has passed the most important Resolution that ever was taken in America," he told James Warren.[1] There could be little doubt that the step tended strongly towards general independence. Yet even now there were others who took a more skeptical or cautious view. Carter Braxton of Virginia informed Landon Carter that the latter would say it fell very little short of independence, but "it was not so understood by the Congress."[2] He admitted, however, that he found people on either side of the question who did now construe it in that sense. He recognized that the assumption of government was necessary. But he also mentioned that the preamble, which declared that all governments deriving their authority from the crown should be "totally suppressed," caused a heated debate lasting two or three days; but Dickinson failed to see the danger, and the Congress, now under strong independent leadership and facing events with a mind to the need for foreign alliances, had gone ahead of the more reluctant colonies.

Maryland continued to exhibit indecision mixed with a desperate hope of reconciliation. Its governing elements, like those of Pennsylvania, contained influential members who dreaded the social upheaval that might follow independence. In New York there was evidence in some quarters of a lingering belief in the arrival of British commissioners. It was Virginia that marked the turning tide. Although some of the Old Dominion's elder statesmen still held back, Jefferson reported that the back country was strongly for independence. The new convention, meeting on May 6, spent a few days in debate, before Patrick Henry (who had briefly held, and resigned, a military commission) stirred them all with a characteristic speech. On May 15, the Provincial Convention voted for independence with only the one dissentient vote of Robert Carter Nicholas. Yet even now a case for delay could be made on grounds of prudence as well as innate conservatism, as Patrick Henry saw when he wrote to John Adams that an alliance with France ought to precede "an open declaration of independency."

In Philadelphia, the Congress continued to make plans for war. There was deep concern about Canada, where military misadventures had not given much indication of the Americans' ability to mount a campaign; in addition to taking further steps to try to secure the Canadian frontier and to gain the respect of the Canadian people, Congress appointed a small committee to confer with the senior generals about strategy. From this meeting came a well-conceived plan for a so-called flying camp in the middle colonies, so placed as to be a base for rapid troop movements wherever they might be needed.

While the radicals now pressed their colleagues in Congress for the final step, men of moderation still urged restraint. The debate that followed when Richard Henry Lee moved formally for American independence on June 7 was not a mere holding action by irreconcilable conservatives. John Adams himself had said to Patrick Henry that he would like to see a colonial confederation, defined by constitutional limits, before announcing that the colonies so confederated formed a sovereign state. Then would be the time for treaties with foreign powers. But he saw that it would be difficult to proceed in such a systematic manner; they would be obliged to declare themselves sovereign states before the confederation had been formed and even before all the colonies had established governments. According to Edward Rutledge of South Carolina, "the sensible part of the House" opposed Lee's motion. He saw no objection to proposing a treaty to France and forming a confederation, but no wisdom in an actual Declaration of Independence, "nor any other purpose to be served by it, but putting ourselves in the power of others with whom we mean to treat, giving our enemy notice of our intentions, and rendering ourselves ridiculous in the eyes of foreign powers by attempting to bring them into a Union before we had united with each other." He mentioned that his allies in this argument were R.R. Livingston, Wilson, and Dickerson (of New Jersey), while the power of New England, Virginia, and Georgia were ranged on the side of independence. Richard Henry Lee, writing to persuade Landon Carter back in Virginia, explained his view: "it is not choice then but necessity that calls for Independence, as the only means by which foreign alliances can be obtained; and a proper Confederation by which peace and union may be secured. We shall not put it in the power of France to hurt us."[3]

On the tenth, the Congress effectively resolved on the need for independence. But it could not yet act. The New York delegates needed to consult their convention; Maryland was still in confusion. The immediate decision was therefore to postpone a declaration for three weeks—until July 1—but in order that no time be lost, a committee was appointed to prepare a draft. The members of this committee were John Adams, Benjamin Franklin,

Roger Sherman, R.R. Livingston, and Thomas Jefferson. The young Virginian, who had keenly impressed the other delegates first by the felicity of his writings, and when they got to know him, by the fluent, informal brilliance of his conversational style, was the last to be appointed to the committee. He took the place of Richard Henry Lee, who wanted to return to take part in events in his own colony. While this committee labored, the Congress moved forward on its other fronts. A committee was set up to prepare a plan for a confederation, and another to prepare the procedure for entering into foreign treaties. Both those were approved on the same day, June 12, an indication of the gathering force of decision and the pace of events.

Meanwhile, the delegates got on with the business as they had been doing for months and as they would continue to do after formally changing their allegiance. The New York Provincial Congress was given recommendations for dealing with disaffected persons, but care was also paid to the need that alleged Tories be treated correctly, as laid down by Congress. The men making this revolution had seen much mob rule and riot, and did not want to loosen the strands of disciplined government and respect for law. The old law and its authorities had to go, however; Governor William Franklin of New Jersey was declared "a virulent enemy" and placed under arrest. Delegates from his province arrived on June 28, with credentials giving them power to join in a declaration of independence—a power which was now clearly lacking only to the delegations from New York and Maryland. Conservatives could do nothing to stop the calendar; as July 1 approached, they could only hope to rally an array of arguments that would against all probability convince the delegates that the possibilities of reconciliation had not yet been exhausted, that the time was not ripe. A preliminary vote on June 30 lacked the support (for some reason) of South Carolina as well as New York and a still hesitant delegation from Pennsylvania; but the majority felt confident that the Pennsylvania delegation were out of touch with their constituents and would very soon swing into line. On July 1, the Maryland Convention at last authorized a vote for independence as Congress assembled to solemnize the final decision and to debate the language in which they would present it to the world.

On June 29, the day after the draft declaration was reported to the Congress by its committee of five, Edward Rutledge wrote to urge John Jay to come down from New York to oppose the forthcoming declaration. Rutledge had been on the committee to draft the preamble to the recommendation for independent governments; so we must infer that he was one of those who did not construe it as leading to independence. These views, which seem ambiguous, can be understood in the light of his belief that state governments could act independently of and without committing Congress. He very much feared the consequences of any further commitment and offered Jay a mordant analysis of the threat to property, order, and social stability. Rutledge, in a vein which would be heard later from a more radical angle of view, expressed his fear of the idea of destroying provincial distinctions and bending everything to "the good of the whole." it meant subjecting them all to "the government of the Eastern provinces"—meaning New England, of whom he spoke with contempt. "I hold their arms cheap, but dread their influence in council," he said. The issue was not merely intercolonial: it was the entire social order. He dreaded, he said, the effects their levelling principles would have on order and on "fluctuation of Property." Congress must be vested with no more power than was absolutely necessary and they—the social leaders—"must keep the staff in our own hands, for I am convinced that if it is surrendered into the hands of others, most pernicious use will be made of it." This striking expression of the "insecure conservative" reasons against independence viewed Congress as a radical instrument.[4] A reversed view prevailed within a few years. Rutledge's doubts, however, did not prevent him from signing the Declaration, as Dickinson's did.

Before the Congress could proceed, Dickinson made a last attempt to deflect their course. In a long, carefully prepared speech he argued again that the plunge into independence, without having composed their own differences or secured the support of the Bourbons, was precipitate and premature. But these arguments had been overtaken by events. If they had been true once, it seemed now that their truth should have been borne out; but every support, every hope on which the reconciliationists had depended had failed them. Dickinson was speaking for a temperament, a frame of mind, rather than a policy. Delegates no doubt listened to him with their accustomed respect, and then got back to business.

## The Declaration

The draft as reported by the committee had undergone a number of alterations (see Document 5-a). Jefferson, to whom the committee had confided the task of preparing the declaration, seems to have shown his first draft only to two other members, Franklin and Adams. A version bearing the alterations made during this period of consultation was first presented to Congress on June 28, when discussion was held over for four days. Most of the early changes were in phraseology rather than substance; but where Jefferson had described the truths of natural law as "sacred and undeniable", another hand, seemingly Franklin's, wrote in "self-evident." This distinctly more secular tone was more than a mere change in form—and it was also more characteristic of Franklin's thought.

The debate on the Declaration was no mere formality. The committee's draft was taken up on July 1 by the Congress sitting as a committee of the whole house, and in that form the delegates scrutinized the words of Jefferson and his colleagues line by line. By the time they had finished, substantial changes had been required.

The most famous excision was of Jefferson's passage against the slave trade. In a complicated paragraph, he managed both to denounce the slave trade and to blame the king for maintaining it, at the same time denouncing him for inciting the slaves themselves to insurrection against their masters. This was not an issue on which South Carolinian and Georgian slaveowners were disposed to risk their reputations; Jefferson also noted afterwards that some northern consciences were touched, not because of slaveownership in the northern colonies, but because of their part in the slave trade. As a result of these objections the whole passage was cut out. So was an unflattering reference to the Scots, whose troops were linked with the Hessians as "foreign mercenaries." One interesting change resulted from differences of view as to the responsibility for the course of British politics. Jefferson sought to blame the British electorate for failing to remove those responsible for American grievances, and also denied that Americans had ever been lawfully subject to Parliament. Even from the colonial standpoint these expressions were contentious. They raised questions of responsibility and of constitutional law on which delegates evidently felt reluctant to commit themselves to so explicit a view. Moreover, the denunciation of the British people was still felt by some to be bad tactics; Jefferson did not agree, but acquiesced. He also tried to date colonial grievances from a specific point—1763. This was the official Virginian view. But it was not consistent with his own attempt to deny the validity of parliamentary sovereignty, which of course had been exercised long before 1763. Intercolonial disputes, already a cause of anxiety in the Congress, turned on the claims to land grants from earlier years; delegates perhaps wisely decided not to tie themselves down.

The Declaration, as finally agreed, fell into two main themes. It began with a preamble, a kind of invocation. In these passages Jefferson sought to gather what may be called the high common sense of contemporary thought about the rights of men as given by the laws of nature. God himself, as conceived by the Deists of the world order as it appeared to the heirs of Newton, was "Nature's God." The laws of moral conduct were nature's laws. Under these laws, all men were thought to be equal—equal in their common possession of human nature and therefore equal in the rights pertaining to that nature. The rights he claimed for them were common rights, easily understood by all, and made familiar in recent years by the reception of John Locke's *Two Treatises of Government*: but since Locke's time, the word "happiness" had come into fashion as a designation of the aim of society and even, to some extent, as a justification for the existence of government. In a brilliant stroke, Jefferson converted Locke's prosaic expression, "Life, liberty and estate" into "Life, liberty and the pursuit of happiness."

The remainder was a long list of the wrongs inflicted on the colonies in the reign of King George III. It represented, in effect, the official bill of complaints, all of which, taken together, proved a dark and carefully matured design to reduce the American colonies to a state of subservience. This list of grievances was formally addressed to "a candid world." But British opinion, repeatedly addressed in the past, had signally failed to respond, and the rest of Europe could hardly have been a primary object of the congressional attention. The truth was that the most important direct object of the rhetoric of the Declaration was not the opinion of the world but of Americans themselves. Many, represented by a respectable and established leadership, had shown marked reluctance to renounce their old loyalties and had opposed Whig leadership, and there were still more whose ultimate commitments, in case of war, could only remain a matter of speculation. The Declaration, with its list of grievances, was a powerful bid for those commitments. Beyond this, the Congress was deeply conscious of its responsibility for upholding the rule of law and fearful of the consequences of lawless action. Indeed the Declaration affirmed that "Governments long established should not be changed for light and transient causes." The structure and argument of the Declaration were intended to prove that the causes were clearly neither light nor transient. To renounce one's allegiance to the Crown was no light matter. Both to convince their constituents and to justify themselves, members of the Congress had need of a catalog of concrete, legally arguable causes for the dissolution of their allegiance—absolving them morally and, they believed, legally, from the taint of treason.

The Declaration had not yet taken its final form when the Congress, on July 2, adopted the resolution that Richard Henry Lee had introduced on June 7. By this act it was resolved "that these United Colonies are, and of right ought to be, free and independent States, that they are absolved from all allegiance to the British Crown, and that all political connection between them and the State of Great Britain is, and ought to be, totally dissolved." This was the irreversible resolution which actually determined American independence; the next day, July 3, John Adams told his wife that "the second day of July 1776 is the most memorable epocha in the history of America." On the fourth, accompanied not inappropriately by thunder and rain, delegates made their way to the hall to adopt the Declaration in its approved form.

The final adoption of the Declaration did not include the ceremony of signing. The New Yorkers could not even subscribe to the vote until their Fourth Provincial Convention gave them authority to do so; meeting on the ninth, that convention agreed to independence as "a cruel necessity"—a very different light from that in which it was viewed by the Adamses or the Lees (see Document 5-b). On July 4, Dickinson, who had earlier voted against independence, did not appear, and neither did Robert Morris. These absences left the Pennsylvania delegates John Morton, Franklin, and Wilson to give an undivided vote. The vote of the colonies on that day was unanimous save for New York—the highest level of unity yet reached. Not until July 19 did the Congress, burdened with urgent business, return to the Declaration and order an engrossed version to be drawn up; and on August 2, the engrossed parchment copy received its ceremonial signatures. These signatures included several—probably seven—who had been absent on July 4; other names were added as new delegates entered the Congress as late as November. Thomas McKean of Delaware, who was present on July 4, but absent on August 2, added his name to the parchment when he returned. In letters written in later years, he alluded to a possibly significant reason for the late signatures when he remarked that he had been told of a resolution entered in the secret journal that no person should be allowed to take his seat until he had signed "in order (as I have been given to understand) to prevent traitors and spies from worming themselves amongst us."

For some fifty men who had been working together for many months in complete personal safety to set their names to a document might seem a commonplace thing. But one signer, Abraham Clark of New Jersey, remarked a few days after reporting the Declaration, that they might all soon be swinging from a high gallows. That would have been an easy death compared with the penalty for high treason, of being hanged, drawn and quartered, which everyone knew had been inflicted on the surviving regicides after the Restoration of Charles II. The colonists knew that admiralty courts had been set up to try Americans without juries, and that a law had been passed by which they could be brought to England to be tried for crimes committed in America. The law knew no greater crime than high treason, and if military defeat followed, the most prominent rebels could hardly expect to plead that they did not know the meaning of their act. In the light of this knowledge, and of all that was at stake, they pledged to each other "our Lives, our Fortunes, and our sacred Honor."

## Notes

1.   Edmund C. Burnett, *Letters*, vol. 1, p. 63.
2.   Ibid., pp. 453-54.
3.   Ibid., pp. 468-69.
4.   Ibid., pp. 517-18.

# Part two

## Documents of the Decision

# 1

# Colonial Resistance Aimed at Redress and Conciliation: The Suffolk Resolves

The Suffolk Resolves, adopted at a meeting in Dedham (then sometimes spelled Deadham) on September 6, 1774, were brought to Philadelphia by Paul Revere on the seventeenth and adopted by the Continental Congress on the same day. The meeting in Dedham claimed to be a county meeting, thereby escaping the British ban on town meetings; but it was a gathering of town representatives, who could hardly have been lawfully elected without contravening the ban in their own towns. The fiery and intemperate language of the preamble to these resolutions makes it particularly interesting that they should have been adopted by the Congress in one day. At almost any later date, the moderates would almost certainly have insisted on a protracted debate; but at this early stage, a mood of enthusiasm combined with genuine sympathy for the sufferings of Boston gave the Massachusetts radicals a momentary advantage, whose momentum they found hard to sustain.

The preamble is important. It served to establish a particular mythology which portrayed the founders of New England and earlier generations of immigrants in the heroic role of persons persecuted for their religion and seeking personal and religious liberty at great risk and self-sacrifice. Of some earlier migrants this was no doubt substantially true. But most of the Britons who crossed the Atlantic were either seeking to improve their fortunes, or were more or less involuntary indentured servants. The view given here, however, had become something of an orthodoxy—which served to put colonists on guard against renewed persecution, either political or religious.

The tone of the Resolves was somewhat at variance with their conclusions. So far as alternatives for action were under consideration, the implications of the passages denouncing the deeds of a "wicked ministry" and the general attribution of tyrannical motives to the British pointed to independence—if the British could not be persuaded to relent. But independence was nowhere mentioned. The full force of the complaint was directed wholly toward the hope of obtaining redress by the repeal of the obnoxious acts of Parliament. But Section 17, which offered submission to whatever measures the Continental Congress chose to adopt, was more than an indication of support: it was a very broad hint that the Congress was expected to take a line of resistance as firm as the tone of the Resolves.

The delegates at Suffolk showed themselves to be aware of the dangers of internal disorder and even of a social collapse. Section 6 urged creditors to show forbearance to their debtors—but of course the meeting could do no more than recommend. Section 18 revealed an understandable fear of violence—for mobs, under careful control, had already done a great deal to disturb the existing authorities. But the time had come to exercise restraint. The leaders of Massachusetts resistance were now facing the problem of responsibility for order when the legal government was breaking down; and when they eventually took their province out of the empire, the future of republican government would depend on their ability to keep order and protect property.

The dispatches from Boston enclosed some resolutions addressed by the Suffolk meeting to General Gage requesting him to dismantle certain military installations that he was putting up at the south entrance to Boston. The resolutions assured Gage that the people of Boston had no warlike intentions against British troops but reminded him of their grievances arising from various provocations including the British action in removing powder from the arsenal at Charlestown. These were printed in the *Journals* but are omitted here.

### *Document*†

SATURDAY, SEPTEMBER 17, 1774, A.M.

The Congress met according to adjournment.

The Resolutions entered into by the delegates from the several towns and districts in the county of Suffolk, in the province of the Massachusetts-bay, on tuesday the 6th instant, and their address to his excellency Gov. Gage, dated the 9th instant, were laid before the congress, and are as follows:

At a meeting of the delegates of every town & district in the county of Suffolk, on tuesday the 6th of Sept$^r$., at the house of M$^r$. Richard Woodward, of Deadham, & by adjournment, at the house of Mr. [Daniel] Vose, of Milton, on Friday the 9th instant, Joseph Palmer, esq. being chosen moderator, and William Thompson, esq. clerk, a committee was chosen to bring in a report to the convention, and the following being several times read, and put paragraph by paragraph, was unanimously voted, viz.

†From: *Journals of the Continental Congress*, vol. 1, pp. 31-37.

Whereas the power but not the justice, the vengeance but not the wisdom of Great-Britain, which of old persecuted, scourged, and exiled our fugitive parents from their native shores, now pursues us, their guiltless children, with unrelenting severity: And whereas, this, then savage and uncultivated desart, was purchased by the toil and treasure, or acquired by the blood and valor of those our venerable progenitors; to us they bequeathed the dearbought inheritance, to our care and protection they consigned it, and the most sacred obligations are upon us to transmit the glorious purchase, unfettered by power, unclogged with shackles, to our innocent and beloved offspring. On the fortitude, on the wisdom and on the exertions of this important day, is suspended the fate of this new world, and of unborn millions. If a boundless extent of continent, swarming with millions, will tamely submit to live, move and have their being at the arbitrary will of a licentious minister, they basely yield to voluntary slavery, and future generations shall load their memories with incessant execrations. On the other hand, if we arrest the hand which would ransack our pockets, if we disarm the parricide which points the dagger to our bosoms, if we nobly defeat that fatal edict which proclaims a power to frame laws for us in all cases whatsoever, thereby entailing the endless and numberless curses of slavery upon us, our heirs and their heirs forever; if we successfully resist that unparalleled usurpation of unconstitutional power, whereby our capital is robbed of the means of life; whereby the streets of Boston are thronged with military executioners; whereby our coasts are lined and harbours crouded with ships of war; whereby the charter of the colony, that sacred barrier against the enroachments of tyranny, is mutilated and, in effect, annihilated; whereby a murderous law is framed to shelter villains from the hands of justice; whereby the unalienable and inestimable inheritance, which we derived from nature, the constitution of Britain, and the privileges warranted to us in the charter of the province, is totally wrecked, annulled, and vacated, posterity will acknowledge that virtue which preserved them free and happy; and while we enjoy the rewards and blessings of the faithful, the torrent of panegyrists will roll our reputations to that latest period, when the streams of time shall be absorbed in the abyss of eternity. Therefore, we have resolved, and do *resolve*,

1. That whereas his majesty, George the Third, is the rightful successor to the throne of Great-Britain, and justly entitled to the allegiance of the British realm, and agreeable to compact, of the English colonies in America therefore, we, the heirs and successors of the first planters of this colony, do cheerfully acknowledge the said George the Third to be our rightful sovereign, and that said covenant is the tenure and claim on which are founded our allegiance and submission.

2. That it is an indispensable duty which we owe to God, our country, ourselves and posterity, by all lawful ways and means in our power to maintain, defend and preserve those civil and religious rights and liberties, for which many of our fathers fought, bled and died, and to hand them down entire to future generations.

3. That the late acts of the British parliament for blocking up the harbour of Boston, for altering the established form of government in this colony, and for screening the most flagitious violators of the laws of the province from a legal trial, are gross infractions of those rights to which we are justly entitled by the laws of nature, the British constitution, and the charter of the province.

4. That no obedience is due from this province to either or any part of the acts above-mentioned, but that they be rejected as the attempts of a wicked administration to enslave America.

5. That so long as the justices of our superior court of judicature, court of assize, &c. and inferior court of common pleas in this county are appointed, or hold their places, by any other tenure than that which the charter and the laws of the province direct, they must be considered as under undue influence, and are therefore unconstitutional officers, and, as such, no regard ought to be paid to them by the people of this county.

6. That if the justices of the superior court of judicature, assize, &c. justices of the court of common pleas, or of the general sessions of the peace, shall sit and act during their present disqualified state, this county will support, and bear harmless, all sheriffs and their deputies, constables, jurors and other officers who shall refuse to carry into execution the orders of said courts; and, as far as possible, to prevent the many inconveniencies which must be occasioned by a suspension of the courts of justice, we do most earnestly recommend it to all creditors, that they shew all reasonable and even generous forbearance to their debtors; and to all debtors, to pay their just debts with all possible speed, and if any disputes relative to debts or trespasses shall arise, which cannot be settled by the parties, we recommend it to them to submit all such causes to arbitration; and it is our opinion that the contending parties or either of them, who shall refuse so to do, ought to be considered as co-operating with the enemies of this country.

7. That it be recommended to the collectors of taxes, constables and all other officers, who have public monies in their hands, to retain the same, and not to make any payment thereof to the provincial county treasurer until the civil government of the province is placed upon a constitutional foundation, or until it shall otherwise be ordered by the proposed provincial Congress.

8. That the persons who have accepted seats at the council board, by virtue of a mandamus from the King, in conformity to the late act of the British parliament, entitled, an act for the regulating the government of the Massachusetts-Bay, have acted in direct violation of the duty they owe to their country, and have thereby given great and just offence to this people; therefore, resolved, that this county do recommend it to all persons, who have so highly offended by accepting said departments, and have not already publicly resigned their seats at the council board, to make public resignations of their places at said board, on or before the 20th day of this instant, September; and that all persons refusing so to do, shall; from and after said day, be considered by this county as obstinate and incorrigible enemies to this country.

9. That the fortifications begun and now carrying on upon Boston Neck, are justly alarming to this county, and gives us reason to apprehend some hostile intention against that town, more especially as the commander in chief has, in a very extraordinary manner, removed the powder from the magazine at Charlestown, and has also forbidden the deeper of the magazine at Boston, to deliver out to the owners, the powder, which they had lodged in said magazine.

10. That the late act of parliament for establishing the Roman Catholic religion and the French laws in that extensive country, now called Canada, is dangerous in an extreme degree to the Protestant religion and to the civil rights and liberties of all America; and, therefore, as men and Protestant Christians, we are indispensably obliged to take all proper measures for our security.

11. That whereas our enemies have flattered themselves that they shall make an easy prey of this numerous, brave and hardy people, from an apprehension that they are unacquainted with military discipline; we, therefore, for the honour, defence and security of this county and province, advise, as it has been recommended to take away all commissions from the officers of the militia, that those who now hold commissions, or such other persons, be elected in each town as officers in the militia, as shall be judged of sufficient capacity for that purpose, and who have evidenced themselves the inflexible friends to the rights of the people; and that the inhabitants of those towns and districts, who are qualified, do use their utmost diligence to acquaint themselves with the art of war as soon as possible, and do, for that purpose, appear under arms at least once every week.

12. That during the present hostile appearances on the part of Great Britain, notwithstanding the many insults and oppressions which we most sensibly resent, yet, nevertheless, from our affection to his majesty, which we have at all times evidenced, we are determined to act merely upon the defensive, so long as such conduct may be vindicated by reason and the principles of self-preservation, but no longer.

13. That, as we understand it has been in contemplation to apprehend sundry persons of this county, who have rendered themselves conspicuous in contending for the violated rights and liberties of their countrymen; we do recommend, should such an audacious measure be put in practice, to seize and keep in safe custody, every servant of the present tyrannical and unconstitutional government throughout the county and province, until the persons so apprehended be liberated from the hands of our adversaries, and restored safe and uninjured to their respective friends and families.

14. That until our rights are fully restored to us, we will, to the utmost of our power, and we recommend the same to the other counties, to withhold all commercial intercourse with Great-Britain, Ireland, and the West-Indies, and abstain from the consumption of British merchandise and manufactures, and especially of East-India teas and piece goods, with such additions, alterations, and exceptions only, as the General Congress of the colonies may agree to.

15. That under our present circumstances, it is incumbent on us to encourage arts and manufactures amongst us, by all means in our power, and that be and are hereby appointed a committee, to consider of the best ways and means to promote and establish the same, and to report to this convention as soon as may be.

16. That the exigencies of our public affairs, demand that a provincial Congress be called to consult such measures as may be adopted, and vigorously executed by the whole people; and we do recommend it to the several towns in this county, to chuse members for such a provincial Congress, to be holden at Concord, on the second Tuesday of October, next ensuing.

17. That this county, confiding in the wisdom and integrity of the continental Congress, now sitting at Philadelphia, pay all due respect and submission to such measures as may be recommended by them to the colonies, for the restoration and establishment of our just rights, civil and religious, and for renewing that harmony and union between Great-Britain and the colonies, so earnestly wished for by all good men.

18. That whereas the universal uneasiness which prevails among all orders of men, arising from the wicked and oppressive measures of the present administration, may influence some unthinking persons to commit outrage upon private property; we would heartily recommend to all persons of this community, not to engage in any routs, riots, or licentious attacks upon the properties of any person whatsoever, as being subversive of all order and government; but, by a steady, manly, uniform, and persevering opposition, to convince our enemies, that in a contest so important, in a cause so solemn, our conduct shall be such as to merit the approbation of the wise, and the admiration of the brave and free of every age and every country.

19. That should our enemies, by any sudden manoeuvres, render it neccessary to ask the aid and assistance of our brethren in the country, some one of the committee of correspondence, or a select man of such town, or the town adjoining, where such hostilities shall commence, or shall be expected to commence, shall despatch couriers with written messages to the select men, or committees of correspondence, of the several towns in the vicinity, with a written account of such matter, who shall despatch others to committees more remote, until proper and sufficient assistance be obtained, and that the expense of said couriers be defrayed by the county, until it shall be otherwise ordered by the provincial Congress.

# 1-a
## Galloway's Plan of Union

Joseph Galloway had very decided ideas about America's Alternatives, and his intense hostility to any suggestion of independence actually gave him more liberty to discuss the subject than was possessed by the radicals who desired it in secret. In this speech he brought the possibility into the open when he said that leading members of Parliament had regarded the resolutions of the Stamp Act Congress as an "explicit declaration of the American Independence." In his second paragraph Galloway set out the propositions so far before Congress—to revert to the status quo that had existed in 1763, and to adopt nonimportation and nonexportation. Since the latter measure was intended to produce the former policy, these constituted a single program. The second major alternative, that of independence, had not yet been officially mentioned in the papers of the Congress and had probably been barely even hinted at in debates. But Galloway now proposed a new and genuinely radical alternative—his Plan of Union. _(1763?)_

At this stage, therefore America had three alternatives to consider: 1: reversion to 1773; 2: Galloway's Plan for a new constitutional Union; or, at the last and if all else failed, 3: Independence.

The constitutional views stated by Galloway in this speech deserve careful study. He was as good a lawyer as his rivals, and grasped the fundamental connection between representation and landownership in the British constitution. Many British Whigs would have concurred. It is interesting to note that Galloway used this connection to argue that not all the acts of Parliament on colonial matters were strictly constitutional.

### Document†

In his *Historical and Political Reflections on the Rise and Progress of the American Rebellion*, Galloway gives the speech he delivered on the motion involving his plan.

Introductory to his motion which led to this plan, the author of it made, in substance, the following speech, which is taken from his short notes: "He told Congress that he came with instructions to propose some mode, by which the harmony between Great-Britain and the Colonies might be restored

†From: *Journals of the Continental Congress*, vol. 1, pp. 44-48.

on constitutional principles: that this appeared to be the genuine sense of all the instructions brought into Congress by the Delegates of the several Colonies. He had long waited with great patience under an expectation of hearing some proposition which should tend to that salutary and important purpose; but, to his great mortification and distress, a month had been spent in fruitless debates on equivocal and indecisive propositions, which tended to inflame rather than reconcile—to produce war instead of peace between the two countries. In this disagreeable situation of things he thought it his incumbent duty to speak plainly, and to give his sentiments without the least reserve.

There are two propositions before the Congress for restoring the wished-for harmony: one, that Parliament should be requested to place the Colonies in the state they were in in the year 1763; the other, that a non-exportation and non-importation agreement should be adopted. I will consider these propositions, and venture to reject them both; the first, as indecisive, tending to mislead both countries, and to lay a foundation for further discontent and quarrel; the other, as illegal, and ruinous to America.

The first proposition is indecisive, because it points out no ground of complaint—asks for a restoration of no right, settles no principle, and proposes no plan for accommodating the dispute. There is no statute which has been passed to tax or bind the Colonies since the year 1763, which was not founded on precedents and statutes of a similar nature before that period; and therefore the proposition, while it expressly denies the right of Parliament, confesses it by the strongest implication. In short, it is nugatory, and without meaning; and however it may serve, when rejected by Parliament, as it certainly will be, to form a charge of injustice upon, and to deceive and inflame the minds of the people hereafter, it cannot possibly answer any other purpose.

The second proposition is undutiful and illegal: it is an insult on the supreme authority of the State; it cannot fail to draw on the Colonies the united resentment of the Mother Country. If we will not trade with Great Britain, she will not suffer us to trade at all. Our ports will be blocked up by British men of war, and troops will be sent to reduce us to reason and obedience. A total and sudden stagnation of commerce is what no country can bear: it must bring ruin on the Colonies: the produce of labour must perish on their hands, and not only the progress of industry be stopped, but industry and labour will cease, and the country itself be thrown into anarchy and tumult. I must therefore reject both the propositions; the first as indecisive, and the other as inadmissible upon any principle of prudence or policy.

If we sincerely mean to accommodate the difference between the two countries, and to establish their union on more firm and constitutional principles, we must take into consideration a number of facts which led the Parliament to pass the acts complained of, since the year 1763, and the real state of the Colonies. A clear and perfect knowledge of these matters only can lead us to the ground of substantial redress and permanent harmony. I will therefore call your recollection to the dangerous situation of the Colonies from the intrigues of France, and the incursions of the Canadians and their Indian allies, at the commencement of the last war. None of us can be ignorant of the just sense they then entertained of that danger, and of their incapacity to defend themselves against it, nor of the supplications made to the Parent State for its assistance, nor of the cheerfulness with which Great-Britain sent over her fleets and armies for their protection, of the millions she expended in that protection, and of the happy consequences which attended it.

In this state of the Colonies, it was not unreasonable to expect that Parliament would have levied a tax on them proportionate to their wealth, and the sums raised in Great Britain. Her ancient right, so often exercised, and never controverted, enabled her, and the occasion invited her, to do it. And yet, not knowing their wealth, a generous tenderness arising from the fear of doing them injustice, induced Parliament to forbear to levy aids upon them. It left the Colonies to do justice to themselves and to the nation. And moreover, in order to allure them to a discharge of their duty, it offered to reimburse those Colonies which should generously grant the aids that were neccessary to their own safety. But what was the conduct of the Colonies on this occasion, in which their own existence was immediately concerned? However painful it may be for me to repeat, or you to hear, I must remind you of it. You all know there were Colonies which at some times granted liberal aids, and at others nothing; other Colonies gave nothing during the war; none gave equitably in proportion to their wealth, and all that did give were actuated by partial and self interested motives, and gave only in proportion to the approach or remoteness of the danger. These delinquencies were occasioned by the want of the exercise of some supreme power to ascertain, with equity, their proportions of aids, and to over-rule the particular passions, prejudices, and interests, of the several Colonies.

To remedy these mischiefs, Parliament was naturally led to exercise the power which had been, by its predecessors, so often exercised over the Colonies, and to pass the Stamp Act. Against this act, the Colonies petitioned Parliament, and denied its authority. Instead of proposing some remedy, by which that authority should be rendered more equitable and more constitutional over the Colonies, the petitions rested in a declaration that the Colonies could not be represented in that body. This justly alarmed the British Senate. It was thought and called by the ablest men and Britain, a clear and explicit declaration of the American Independence, and compelled the Parliament to pass the Declaratory Act, in order to save its ancient and incontrovertible right of supremacy over all the parts of the empire. By this injudicious step the cause of our complaints became fixed, and instead of obtaining a constitutional reformation of the authority of Parliament over the Colonies, it brought on an explicit declaration of a right in Parliament to exercise absolute and unparticipated power over them. Nothing now can be wanting to convince us, that the Assemblies have pursued measures which have produced no relief, and answered no purpose but a bad one. I therefore hope that the collected wisdom of Congress will perceive and avoid former mistakes; that they will candidly and thoroughly examine the real merits of our dispute with the Mother Country, and take such ground as shall firmly unite us under one system of polity, and make us one people.

In order to establish those principles, upon which alone American relief ought, in reason and policy, to be founded, I will take a brief view of the arguments on both sides of the great question between the two countries—a question in its magnitude and importance exceeded by none that has been ever agitated in the councils of any nation. The advocates for the supremacy of Parliament over the Colonies contend, that there must be one supreme legislative head in every civil society, whose authority must extend to the regulation and final decision of every matter susceptible of human direction; and that every member of the society, whether political, official, or individual, must be subordinate to its supreme will, signified in its laws: that this supremacy and subordination are essential in the constitution of all States, whatever may be their forms; that no society ever did or could exist, without it; and that these truths are solidly established in the practice of all governments, and confirmed by the concurrent authority of all writers on the subject of civil society.

These advocates also assert, what we cannot deny—That the discovery of the Colonies was made under a commission granted by the supreme authority of the British State, that they have been settled under that authority, and therefore are truly the property of that State. Parliamentary jurisdiction has been constantly exercised over them from their first settlement; its executive authority has ever run through all their inferior political systems: the Colonists have ever sworn allegiance to the British State, and have been considered, both by the State and by themselves, as subjects of the British Government. Protection and allegiance are reciprocal duties; the one cannot exist without the other. The Colonies cannot claim the protection of Britain upon any principle of reason or law, while they deny its supreme authority. Upon this ground the authority of Parliament stands too firm to be shaken by any arguments whatever; and therefore to deny that authority, and at the same time to declare their incapacity to be represented, amounts to a full and explicit declaration of independence.

In regard to the political state of the Colonies, you must know that they are so many inferior societies, disunited and unconnected in polity. That while they deny the authority of Parliament, they are, in respect to each other, in a perfect state of nature, destitute of any supreme direction or decision whatever, and incompetent to the grant of national aids, or any other general measure whatever, even to the settlement of differences among themselves. This they have repeatedly acknowledged, and particularly by their delegates in Congress in the Beginning of the last war; and the aids granted by them since that period, for their own protection, are a proof of the truth of that acknowledgment.

You also knew that the seeds of discord are plentifully sowed in the constitution of the Colonies; that they are already grown to maturity, and have more than once broke out into open hostilities. They are at this moment only suppressed by the authority of the Parent State; and should that authority be weakened or annulled, many subjects of unsettled disputes, and which in that case, can only be settled by an appeal to the sword must involve us in all the horrors of civil war. You will now consider whether you wish to be destitute of the protection of Great Britain, or to see a renewal of the claims of France upon America; or to remain in our present disunited state, the weak exposed to the force of the strong. I am sure no honest man can entertain wishes so ruinous to his country.

Having thus briefly stated the arguments in favour of parliamentary authority, and considered the state of the Colonies, I am free to confess that the exercise of that authority is not perfectly constitutional in respect to the Colonies. We know that the whole landed interest of Britain is represented in that body, while neither the land nor the people of America hold the least participation in the legislative authority of the State. Representation, or a participation in the supreme councils of the State, is the great principle upon which the freedom of the British Government is established and secured. I also acknowledge, that that territory whose people have no enjoyment of this privilege, are subject to an authority unrestrained and absolute; and if the liberty of the subject were not essentially concerned in it, I should reject a distinction so odious between members of the same state, so long as it shall be continued. I wish to see it exploded, and the right to participate in the supreme councils of the State extended, in some form, not only to America, but to all the British dominions; otherwise I fear that profound and excellent fabrick of civil polity will, ere long, crumble to pieces.

The case of the Colonies is not a new one. It was formerly the very situation of Wales, Durham and Chester.

As to the tax, it is neither unjust or oppressive, it being rather a relief than a burthen; but it is want of constitutional principle in the authority that passed it, which is the ground for complaint. This, and this only, is the source of American grievances. Here, and here only, is the defect; and if this defect were removed, a foundation would be laid for the relief of every American complaint; the obnoxious statutes would of course be repealed, and others would be made, with the assent of the Colonies, to answer the same and better purposes; the mischiefs arising from the disunion of the Colonies would be removed; their freedom would be established, and their subordination fixed on solid constitutional principles.

Desirous as I am to promote the freedom of the Colonies, and to prevent the mischiefs which will attend a military contest with Great-Britain, I must intreat you to desert the measures which have been so injudiciously and ineffectually pursued by antecedent Assemblies. Let us thoroughly investigate the subject matter in dispute, and endeavour to find from that investigation the means of perfect and permanent redress. In whatever we do, let us be particular and explicit, and not wander in general allegations. These will lead us to no point, nor can produce any relief; they are besides dishonourable and insidious. I would therefore acknowledge the neccessity of the supreme authority of Parliament over the Colonies, because it is a proposition which we cannot deny without manifest contradiction, while we confess that we are subjects of the British Government; and if we do not approve of a representation in Parliament, let us ask for a participation in the freedom and power of the English constitution in some other mode of incorporation: for I am convinced, by long attention to the subject, that let us deliberate, and try what other expedients we may, we shall find none that can give to the Colonies substantial freedom, but some such incorporation. I therefore beseech you, by the respect you are bound to pay to the instructions of your constituents, by the regard you have for the honour and safety of your country, and as you wish to avoid a war with Great-Britain, which must terminate, at all events in the ruin of America, not to rely on a denial of the authority of Parliament, a refusal to be represented, and on a non-importation agreement; because whatever protestations, in that case, may be made to the contrary, it will prove to the world that we intend to throw off our allegiance to the State, and to involve the two countries in all the horrors of a civil war.

With a view to promote the measure I have so earnestly recommended, I have prepared the draught of a plan for uniting America more intimately, in constitutional policy, with Great Britain. It contains the great outlines or principles only, and will require many additions in case those should be approved. I am certain when dispassionately considered, it will be found to be the most perfect union in power and liberty with the Parent State, next to a representation in Parliament, and I trust it will be approved of by both countries. In forming it, I have been particularly attentive to the rights of both; and I am confident that no American, who wishes to continue a subject of the British State, which is what we all uniformly profess, can offer any reasonably objection against it.

I shall not enter into a further explanation of its principles, but shall reserve my sentiments until the second reading, with which I hope it will be favoured."

The introductory motion being seconded, the Plan was presented and read. Warm and long debates immediately ensued on the question, Whether it should be entered in the proceedings of Congress, or be referred to further consideration. All the men of property, and most of the ablest speakers, supported the motion, while the republican party strenuously opposed it.

The question was at length carried by a majority of one Colony.


From Galloway, *Historical and Political Reflections on the Rise and Progress of the American Rebellion*, (1780), 70.

## The Plan

That the several assemblies shall choose members for the grand council in the following proportions, viz.

| | |
|---|---|
| New Hampshire. | Delaware Counties. |
| Massachusetts-Bay. | Maryland. |
| Rhode Island. | Virginia. |
| Connecticut. | North Carolina. |
| New-York. | South-Carolina. |
| New-Jersey. | Georgia. |
| Pennsylvania. | |

Who shall meet at the city of          for the first time, being called by the President-General, as soon as conveniently may be after his appointment.

That there shall be a new election of members for the Grand Council every three years; and on the death, removal or resignation of any member, his place shall be supplied by a new choice, at the next sitting of Assembly of the Colony he represented.

That the Grand Council shall meet once in every year, if they shall think it necessary, and oftener, if occasions shall require, at such time and place as they shall adjourn to, at the last preceding meeting, or as they shall be called to meet at, by the President-General, on any emergency.

That the Grand Council shall have power to choose their Speaker, and shall hold and exercise all the like rights, liberties and privileges, as are held and exercised by and in the House of Commons of Great-Britain.

That the President-General shall hold his office during the pleasure of the King, and his assent shall be requisite to all acts of the Grand Council, and it shall be his office and duty to cause them to be carried into execution.

That the President-General, by and with the advice and consent of the Grand-Council, hold and exercise all the legislative rights, powers, and authorities, necessary for regulating and administering all the general police and affairs of the colonies, in which Great-Britain and the colonies, or any of them, the colonies in general, or more than one colony, are in any manner concerned, as well civil and criminal as commercial.

That the said President-General and the Grand Council, be an inferior and distinct branch of the British legislature, united and incorporated with it, for the aforesaid general purposes; and that any of the said general regulations may originate and be formed and digested, either in the Parliament of Great Britain, or in the said Grand Council, and being prepared, transmitted to the other for their approbation or dissent; and that the assent of both shall be requisite to the validity of all such general acts or statutes.

That in time of war, all bills for granting aid to the crown, prepared by the Grand Council, and approved by the President General, shall be valid and passed into a law, without the assent of the British Parliament.

# ══════════ The Colonial Association

The Association represented the agreements reached through some six weeks of debate. The acrimonious nature of some of the exchanges cannot be detected in the language of the Association. But the notable provision in Section 3 which exempted South Carolina's rice exports from the proposed general ban to date from September 10, 1775, was reached only after severe altercations about distribution of the sacrifices. When all the differences of region and interest as well as social structures are considered, however, the remarkable thing is the extent of the agreement. It was achieved by placing all the hopes and directing all the energies of the Congress toward forcing the British government to redress American grievances and restore the ancient harmony (*Alternative 1-b*). Since Galloway's plan had been decisively rejected, America, so far as its avowed aims were concerned, now had no alternatives. It had one aim and one only—to secure British concessions within the empire. The alternative, of course, was independence, but that was kept out of sight, and as far as most members of the Congress were concerned, out of mind too.

The Association nevertheless took important steps toward the assumption of responsibilities usually connected with government. Sections 11, 12, and 14 arranged for a system of enforcement throughout the continent, and in section 14 the Congress took it upon itself to bind not only its own members but its constituents to the observation of the articles agreed upon. By what authority?—opponents might ask. The answer could only be that the Association, in imposing involuntary requirements on his majesty's colonial subjects, was the first step in a progress toward the transfer of power. While aiming at conciliation, by this measure the Congress took its first step toward a revolution in the basis of authority in America.

*Document†*

## THURSDAY, OCTOBER 20, 1774.

The Congress met.

The association being copied, was read and signed at the table, and is as follows:—

†From: *Journals of the Continental Congress*, vol. 1, pp. 75-80.

Here insert the Association.

WE, his majesty's most loyal subjects, the delegates of the several colonies of New-Hampshire, Massachusetts-Bay, Rhode-Island, Connecticut, New-York, New-Jersey, Pennsylvania, the three lower counties of New-Castle, Kent and Sussex, on Delaware, Maryland, Virginia, North-Carolina, and South-Carolina, deputed to represent them in a continental Congress, held in the city of Philadelphia, on the 5th day of September, 1774, avowing our allegiance to his majesty, our affection and regard for our fellow-subjects in Great-Britain and elsewhere, affected with the deepest anxiety, and most alarming apprehensions, at those grievances and distresses, with which his Majesty's American subjects are oppressed; and having taken under our most serious deliberation, the state of the whole continent, find, that the present unhappy situation of our affairs is occasioned by a ruinous system of colony administration, adopted by the British ministry about the year 1763, evidently calculated for inslaving these colonies, and, with them, the British empire. In prosecution of which system, various acts of parliament have been passed, for raising a revenue in America, for depriving the American subjects, in many instances, of the constitutional trial by jury, exposing their lives to danger, by directing a new and illegal trial beyond the seas, for crimes alleged to have been committed in America: and in prosecution of the same system, several late, cruel, and oppressive acts have been passed, respecting the town of Boston and the Massachusetts Bay, and also an act for extending the province of Quebec, so as to border on the western frontiers of these colonies, establishing an arbitrary government therein, and discouraging the settlement of British subjects in that wide extended country; thus, by the influence of civil principles and ancient prejudices, to dispose the inhabitants to act with hostility against the free Protestant colonies, whenever a wicked ministry shall chuse so to direct them.

To obtain redress of these grievances, which threaten destruction to the lives, liberty, and property of his majesty's subjects, in North America, we are of opinion, that a non-importation, non-consumption, and non-exportation agreement, faithfully adhered to, will prove the most speedy, effectual, and peaceable measure: and, therefore, we do, for ourselves, and the inhabitants of the several colonies, whom we represent, firmly agree and associate, under the sacred ties of virtue, honour and love of our country, as follows:

1. That from and after the first day of December next, we will not import, into British America, from Great-Britain or Ireland, any goods, wares, or merchandise whatsoever, or from any other place, any such goods, wares, or merchandise, as shall have been exported from Great-Britain or Ireland; nor will we, after that day, import any East-India tea from any part of the world; nor any molasses, syrups, paneles, [brown unpurified sugar] coffee, or pimento, from the British plantations or from Dominica; nor wines from Madeira, or the Western Islands; nor foreign indigo.

2. We will neither import nor purchase, any slave imported after the first day of December next; after which time, we will wholly discontinue the slave

trade, and will neither be concerned in it ourselves, nor will we hire our vessels, nor sell our commodities or manufactures to those who are concerned in it.

3. As a non-consumption agreement, strictly adhered to, will be an effectual security for the observation of the non-importation, we, as above, solemnly agree and associate, that, from this day, we will not purchase or use any tea, imported on account of the East-India company, or any on which a duty hath been or shall be paid; and from and after the first day of March next, we will not purchase or use any East-India tea whatever; nor will we, nor shall any person for or under us, purchase or use any of those goods, wares, or merchandise, we have agreed not to import, which we shall know, or have cause to suspect, were imported after the first day of December, except such as come under the rules and directions of the tenth article hereafter mentioned.

4. The earnest desire we have, not to injure our fellow-subjects in Great-Britain, Ireland, or the West-Indies, induces us to suspend a non-exportation, until the tenth day of September, 1775; at which time, if the said acts and parts of acts of the British parliament herein after mentioned are not repealed, we will not, directly or indirectly, export any merchandise or commodity whatsoever to Great-Britain, Ireland, or the West-Indies, except rice to Europe.

5. Such as are merchants, and use the British and Irish trade, will give orders, as soon as possible, to their factors, agents and correspondents, in Great-Britain and Ireland, not to ship any goods to them, on any pretence whatsoever, as they cannot be received in America; and if any merchant, residing in Great-Britain or Ireland, shall directly or indirectly ship any goods, wares or merchandise, for America, in order to break the said non-importation agreement, or in any manner contravene the same, on such unworthy conduct being well attested, it ought to be made public; and, on the same being so done, we will not, from thenceforth, have any commercial connexion with such merchant.

6. That such as are owners of vessels will give positive orders to their captains, or masters, not to receive on board their vessels any goods prohibited by the said non-importation agreement, on pain of immediate dismission from their service.

7. We will use our utmost endeavours to improve the breed of sheep, and increase their number to the greatest extent; and to that end, we will kill them as seldom as may be, especially those of the most profitable kind; nor will we export any to the West-Indies or elsewhere; and those of us, who are or may become overstocked with, or can conveniently spare any sheep, will dispose of them to our neighbours, especially to the poorer sort, on moderate terms.

8. We will, in our several stations, encourage frugality, economy, and industry, and promote agriculture, arts and the manufactures of this country, especially that of wool; and will discountenance and discourage every species of extravagance and dissipation, especially all horse-racing, and all kinds of

gaming, cock-fighting, exhibitions of shews, plays, and other expensive diversions and entertainments; and on the death of any relation or friend, none of us, or any of our families, will go into any further mourning-dress, than a black crape or ribbon on the arm or hat, for gentlemen, and a black ribbon and necklace for ladies, and we will discontinue the giving of gloves and scarves at funerals.

9. Such as are venders of goods or merchandise will not take advantage of the scarcity of goods, that may be occasioned by this association, but will sell the same at the rates we have been respectively accustomed to do, for twelve months last past.—And if any vender of goods or merchandise shall sell any such goods on higher terms, or shall, in any manner, or by any device whatsoever violate or depart from this agreement, no person ought, nor will any of us deal with any such person, or his or her factor or agent, at any time thereafter, for any commodity whatever.

10. In case any merchant, trader, or other person, shall import any goods or merchandise, after the first day of December, and before the first day of February next, the same ought forthwith, at the election of the owner, to be either re-shipped or delivered up to the committee of the county or town, wherein they shall be imported, to be stored at the risque of the importer, until the non-importation agreement shall cease, or be sold under the direction of the committee aforesaid; and in the last-mentioned case, the owner or owners of such goods shall be reimbursed out of the sales, the first cost and charges, the profit, if any, to be applied towards relieving and employing such poor inhabitants of the town of Boston, as are immediate sufferers by the Boston port-bill; and a particular account of all goods so returned, stored, or sold, to be inserted in the public papers; and if any goods or merchandises shall be imported after the said first day of February, the same ought forthwith to be sent back again, without breaking any of the packages thereof.

11. That a committee be chosen in every county, city, and town, by those who are qualified to vote for representatives in the legislature, whose business it shall be attentively to observe the conduct of all persons touching this association; and when it shall be made to appear, to the satisfaction of a majority of any such committee, that any person within the limits of their appointment has violated this association, that such majority do forthwith cause the truth of the case to be published in the gazette; to the end, that all such foes to the rights of British-America may be publicly known, and universally contemned as the enemies of American liberty; and thenceforth we respectively will break off all dealings with him or her.

12. That the committee of correspondence, in the respective colonies, do frequently inspect the entries of their custom-houses, and inform each other, from time to time, of the true state thereof, and of every other material circumstance that may occur relative to this association.

13. That all manufactures of this country be sold at reasonable prices, so that no undue advantage be taken of a future scarcity of goods.

14. And we do further agree and resolve, that we will have no trade,

commerce, dealings or intercourse whatsoever, with any colony or province, in North-America, which shall not accede to, or which shall hereafter violate this association, but will hold them as unworthy of the rights of freemen, and as inimical to the liberties of their country.

And we do solemnly bind ourselves and our constituents, under the ties aforesaid, to adhere to this association, until such parts of the several acts of parliament passed since the close of the last war, as impose or continue duties on tea, wine, molasses, syrups, paneles, coffee, sugar, pimento, indigo, foreign paper, glass, and painters' colours, imported into America, and extend the powers of the admiralty courts beyond their ancient limits, deprive the American subject of trial by jury, authorize the judge's certificate to indemnify the prosecutor from damages, that he might otherwise be liable to from a trial by his peers, require oppressive security from a claimant of ships or goods seized, before he shall be allowed to defend his property, are repealed.—And until that part of the act of the 12 G. 3. ch. 24, entitled "An act for the better securing his majesty's dock-yards, magazines, ships, ammunition, and stores," by which any persons charged with committing any of the offences therein described, in America, may be tried in any shire or county within the realm, is repealed—and until the four acts, passed the last session of parliament, viz. that for stopping the port and blocking up the harbour of Boston—that for altering the charter and government of the Massachusetts-Bay—and that which is entitled "An act for the better administration of justice, &c."—and that "for extending the limits of Quebec, &c." are repealed. And we recommend it to the provincial conventions, and to the committees in the respective colonies, to establish such farther regulations as they may think proper, for carrying into execution this association.

The foregoing association being determined upon by the Congress, was ordered to be subscribed by the several members thereof; and thereupon, we have hereunto set our respective names accordingly.

IN CONGRESS, PHILADELPHIA, *October 20, 1774.*

Signed,                              PEYTON RANDOLPH, *President.*

| *New Hampshire* | Jn.º Sullivan | | J. Kinsey |
| | Nath.el Folsom | | Wil: Livingston |
| | Thomas Cushing | New Jersey | Step.n Crane |
| Massachusetts Bay | Sam.l Adams | | Rich.d Smith |
| | John Adams | | John De Hart |
| | Rob.t Treat Paine | | Jos. Galloway |
| Rhode Island | Step. Hopkins | | John Dickinson |
| | Sam: Ward | | Cha Humphreys |
| | Elipht Dyer | Pennsylvania | Thomas Mifflin |
| Connecticut | Roger Sherman | | E. Biddle |
| | Silas Deane | | John Morton |
| | Isaac Low | | Geo: Ross |
| | John Alsop | The Lower | Caesar Rodney |
| | John Jay | Counties | Tho. M: Kean |

|            |                   | New Castle | Geo: Read              |
|------------|-------------------|------------|------------------------|
| New York   | Ja.ˢ Duane        |            | Mat Tilghman           |
|            | Phil. Livingston  |            | Th.ˢ Johnson Jun.ʳ     |
|            | W.ᵐ Floyd         | Maryland   | W.ᵐ Paca               |
|            | Henry Wisner      |            | Samuel Chase           |
|            | S: Boerum         |            |                        |

*Nor Carolina didn't sign?*

*Omitted p. 81*

# 2

# Lord North's
# Olive Branch

This proposition, often called Lord North's olive branch, was duly entered in the *Journals of the Congress*, from which it is reprinted here with the editorial footnote which gives useful background information.

For reasons explained in the text (pp. 00) the proposition (which actually arrived in Philadelphia at almost the same moment as the news of Lexington and Concord) was constitutionally unacceptable to the Congress. Even the conciliationists found it hard to concur with the principle that Parliament should dispose of funds raised by colonial taxation.

*Document†*
*Copy of a Resolution of the House of Commons, Feb$^y$ 20, 1775.[1]*
*Resolved.* That when the governor, council and Assembly, or general Court, of any of his Majesty's provinces, or colonies, in America, shall propose to make provision according to the condition, circumstances, and

†From: *Journals of the Continental Congress*, vol. 2, pp. 62-63.

[1] On the last day of September, 1774, writs were issued for a new election. The action was unexpected, and is believed to have been taken in order that the petition and other papers of the American Congress might not be received in a Parliament which, however favorable to the existing ministry, might be made even stronger in its interest. The King and Lord North took the keenest interest in the elections for the new Parliament, and the system of election admitted of such manipulation as to ensure a majority in favor of the government. Seats were at the command of the highest bidder, and costly as it was, a House under the control of the ministry was obtained. The King desired the House to contain "gentlemen of landed property," as the "Nabobs, Planters, and other Volunteers are not ready for the battle." *To Lord North*, 24 August, 1774. The policy of the King had been determined. The colonies must submit or triumph. "I do not wish to come to severer measures, but we must not retreat; by coolness and an unremitted pursuit of the measures that have been adopted I trust they will come to submit; I have no objection afterwards to their seeing that there is no inclination for the present to lay fresh taxes on them, but I am clear there must always be one tax to keep up the right, and as such I approve of the Tea Duty." *To Lord North*, 11 September, 1774.

The new Parliament assembled November 30, 1774, and the King's speech spoke of the continued daring spirit of resistance to the laws in America, which in Massachusetts Bay had broken forth in fresh violences of a very criminal nature, and was countenanced and encouraged in other colonies. He declared his resolution to withstand every attempt to weaken or impair the supreme authority of the legislature over all his dominions, the maintenance of which he considered essential to the dignity, safety and welfare of the empire. It was at this time that Franklin wrote an "intended speech" for the opening of the Parliament (*Nation*, 9 February, 1899). The address favorable to the Ministry was situation of such province or colony, for contributing their proportion to the common defence, (such proportion to be raised under the authority of the general court, or general assembly of such province or colony, and disposable by parliament,) and shall engage to make provision also for the support of the civil government, and the administration of Justice, in such province or colony, it will be proper, if such proposal shall be approved by his Majesty, and the two houses of Parliament, and for so long as such provision shall be made accordingly, to forbear, in respect of such province or colony, to levy any duty, tax or assessment, or to impose any further duty, tax, or assessment, except only such duties as it may be expedient to continue to levy, or to impose, for the regulation of commerce, the net produce of the duties, last mentioned, to be carried to the account of such province, or colony, respectively.

*Ordered*, That the above be referred to the committee for taking into consideration the state of America.

carried in both houses, and the Parliament adjourned on December 19, to reassemble on January 19, 1775, when the Papers relating to the "Disturbances in North America" were laid before the House, by his Majesty's command, and referred to the consideration of a committee of the whole House on January 26. In the Lords the papers were received on January 20, and on the next day, Lord Chatham, without having consulted any of his party or followers, made his motion for withdrawing the troops from Boston. The motion was thrown out by a vote of 68 to 18, and early in February the bill for restraining the trade and commerce of the New England colonies was laid before the House, and three Major-Generals had been selected to be sent to America. The Petition of Congress to the King had received no notice except to be included in the mass of papers sent to Parliament, and the well intentioned efforts to obtain from Franklin some definite propositions of compromise and his personal aid in urging them upon the Colonies had produced no results.

Two days after Parliament had assembled, on January 21, the King's Cabinet had met at the house of the Earl of Sandwich, with the following members present: the Lord Chancellor; the Lord President, the Earls of Sandwich, Dartmouth, Suffolk, Rochford and Lord North. It was agreed "that an address be proposed to the two Houses of Parliament to declare that if the Colonies shall make sufficient and permanent provision for the support of the civil government and administration of justice, and for the defence and protection of the said Colonies, and in time of war contribute extraordinary supplies in a reasonable proportion to what is raised by Great Britain, we will in that case desist from the exercise of the power of taxation, except for commercial purposes only, and that whenever a proposition of this kind shall be made by any of the Colonies we will enter into the consideration of proper laws for that purpose, and in the mean while to entreat his Majesty to take the most effectual methods to enforce due obedience to the laws and authority of the supreme legislature of Great Britain." Minute of Meeting in *Dartmouth Manuscripts.* This is the first form of what came to be known as Lord North's motion of reconciliation, adopted by Parliament on February 20.

The motion was sent to the Colonial Governors in a circular letter from Lord Dartmouth, 3 March, 1775. This letter is printed in the *New Jersey Archives*, First Series, X, 555. It was submitted to the General Assembly of Pennsylvania by Governor John Penn, 2 May, 1775, and is printed, together with the reply of the Assembly, in the *Pennsylvania Packet*, 8 May, 1775.

# 3

# War: Declaration Of Causes Of Taking Up Arms

When the Congress decided to raise an army and appoint a commander in chief in the person of George Washington, the time had come for a statement of purpose. The aim was not only to explain these actions to the British government and people. There were many Americans who remained unconvinced, bewildered, and potentially even hostile to the course of resistance. The most imperative need of the Congress was to secure the support and cooperation of the colonists, for without a genuine willingness to support the continental army and to enforce the decrees of the Congress and of the local committees, the struggle against Britain would be bound to fail.

The process of drafting this declaration was not easy. The editorial footnotes to the published *Journals* are reproduced here to explain the background. The editor of the *Journals* reproduced Jefferson's drafts, the second of which bore corrections apparently by Dickinson, before giving Dickinson's draft, followed by the declaration as finally adopted. For reasons of space we reproduce here only Jefferson's second draft followed by the final form. For further information the reader should turn to Julian P. Boyd et al., eds., *The Papers of Thomas Jefferson* (Princeton University Press: 1950), vol. 1, pp. 187-219. Jefferson's drafts were never adopted, but they help to explain how the declaration took its final form.

The two remaining alternatives were clearly struggling with each other in the very process by which the declaration was composed. Basically, Jefferson now looked toward independence if the combined force of economic sanctions and military resistance failed to bring the British to terms. Dickinson simply refused to look beyond the long-term effects of these measures. They must be persisted with until they *did* bring the British to terms. Hence, even while resisting by force of arms, the author of the *Farmer's Letters* felt that it was of the utmost importance to continue to woo the British with the language of conciliation and loyalty. This entire attitude, as we have seen, disgusted John Adams, but the fact remains that Congress preferred it.

## Document†

### Declaration on Taking Arms.[1]
### JEFFERSON'S DRAFTS[2]

First Draft.                             Second Draft.

A Declaration by
We the representatives of the
United Colonies of America now
sitting in General Congress, to all
nations send greeting of setting forth
the causes and necessity of their taking
up arms.

*NB*

---

†From: *Journals of the Continental Congress*, vol. 2, pp. 128-57.

[1] The Committee appointed to draw up a Declaration to be published by General Washington, upon his arrival at the Camp before Boston, reported a draft on June 24th, which occasioned long and warm debate, and was finally re-committed. No copy of this first draft said, by Jefferson, to have been drawn by John Rutledge, is known to exist. Dickinson had taken a distinguished part of this debate, and with Jefferson was added to the Committee. Jefferson was desired to prepare a draft, but the result was not satisfactory either to Dickinson or to William Livingston. The former criticised it for its harshness, and the latter for its "much fault-finding and declamation, with little sense or dignity. They seem to think a reiteration of tyranny, despotism, bloody, &c. all that is needed to unite us at home and convince the bribed voters of North of the justice of our cause." (*Letter to Lord Stirling*, July 4, 1775.) Jefferson's own account was: "It was too strong for Mr. Dickinson. He still retained the hope of reconciliation with the mother country, and was unwilling it should be lessened by offensive statements. He was so honest a man, and so able a one, that he was greatly indulged even by those who could not feel his scruples. We therefore requested him to take the paper, and put it into a form he could approve. He did so, preparing an entire new statement, and preserving of the former only the last four paragraphs and the half of the preceding one. We approved and reported it to Congress." *Autobiography*, in *Writings* (Ford) I, 16.

[2] These two papers are found in the Jefferson Manuscripts in the Library of Congress. The second, or later, draft contains some suggested changes in the writing of John Dickinson, and bears on the last page the following memorandum by Jefferson:

"1775, June 23. Congress appointed a commee to prepare a Declaration to be published by Gen. Washington on his arrival at the camp before Boston, to wit, J. Rutledge, W. Livingston, Dr. Franklin, Mr. Jay, and Mr. Johnson.

"June 24, a draught was reported.

"June 26, being disliked, it was recommitted and Mr. Dickinson and T. Jefferson added to the committee. The latter being desired by the commee to draw up a new one, he prepared this paper. on a meeting of the commee J. Dickinson objected that it was too harsh, wanted softening, &c., whereupon the commee desired him to retouch it, which he did in the form which they reported July 6, which was adopted by Congress."

The large strides of late taken by the *legislature of Great Britain* towards establishing over these colonies their absolute rule, and the hardiness of the present attempt to effect by force of arms what by law or right they could never effect, *render* it neccessary for us also to change the ground of opposition, and to close with their last appeal from reason to arms. And as it behoves those, who *are called to this great decision*, to be assured that their cause is approved before supreme reason; so is it of great avail that it's justice be made known to the world, whose affections will ever take part with those encountering oppression. Our forefathers, inhabitants of the island of Great Britain, [having long endeavored to bear up against the evils of misrule,] left their native land to seek on these shores a residence for civil and religious freedom. At the expence of their blood, [with] to the ruin of their fortunes, with the relinquishment of everything quiet and comfortable in life, they effected settlements in the inhospitable wilds of America; [they] and there established civil societies with various forms of constitution. [But possessing all, what is inherent in all, the full and perfect powers of legislation]. To continue their connection with the friends whom they had left, they arranged themselves by charters of compact under one the same common king, who thus completed their powers of full and perfect legislation and became the link of union between the several parts of the empire. Some occasional assumptions of power by the parliament of Great Britain, however unacknowledged by the constitution of our governments, were finally acquiesced in thro' warmth of affection. Proceeding thus in the fullness of mutual harmony and confidence, both parts of the empire increased in population and in wealth with a rapidity unknown in the history of man. The political institutions of America, it's various soils and climates opened a certain resource to the unfortunate and to the enterprising of every country, and ensured to them the acquisition and free possession of property. Great Britain too acquired a lustre and a weight among the powers of the earth which her internal resources could never have given her. To a communication of the wealth and the power of [the whole] every part of the empire we may surely ascribe in some measure the illustrious character she sustained through her last European war, and its successful event. At the close of that war [however having subdued all her foes[1]] it pleased our sovereign to make a change in his counsels. The new ministry finding all the foes of Britain subdued she took up the unfortunate idea of subduing her friends also,[2] her parliament then for the first time [asserted a right[3]] assumed a power of unbounded legislation over the colonies of America; and in the [space] course of ten years [during which they have proceeded to exercise this right,] have given such decisive specimen of the spirit of this new legislation, as leaves no room to doubt the consequence of acquiescence under it.

[1] John Dickinson has here interlined "her successful and glorious minister was."
[2] Dickinson has inserted "by their influence."
[3] Dickinson changes it to read "were persuaded to assume and assert."

By several acts of parliament passed within that [space of] time they have [attempted to take from us] undertaken to give and grant our money without our consent: a right of which we have ever had the exclusive exercise; they have interdicted all commerce to one of our principal towns, thereby annihilating it's property in the hands of the holders; they have cut off the commercial intercourse of whole colonies with foreign countries; they have extended the jurisdiction of courts of admiralty beyond their antient limits; [thereby] they have deprived us of the inestimable [right] privilege of trial by a jury of the vicinage in cases affecting both life and property; they have declared that American Subjects charged with certain offenses shall be transported beyond sea to be tried before the very persons against whose pretended sovereignty the offense is supposed to be committed; they have attempted fundamentally to alter the form of government in one of these colonies, a form [established] secured by charters on the part of the crown and confirmed by acts of it's own legislature; [and further secured by charters on the part of the crown;] they have erected in a neighboring province, acquired by the joint arms of Great Britain and America, a tyranny dangerous to the very existence of all these colonies. But why should we enumerate their injuries in the detail? By one act they have suspended the powers of one American legislature, and by another have declared they may legislate for us themselves in all cases whatsoever. These two acts alone form a basis broad enough whereon to erect a despotism of unlimited extent. And what is to secure us against this dreaded evil? The persons assuming these powers are not chosen by us, are not subject to our controul or influence, are exempted by their situation from the operation of these laws, and lighten their own burthens in proportion as they increase ours. These temptations might put to trial the severest characters of antient virtue: with what new armour then shall a British parliament encounter the rude assault? to ward these deadly injuries from the tender plant of liberty which we have brought over, and with so much affection fostered on these our own shores, we have pursued every temperate, every respectful measure. We have supplicated our king at various times, in terms almost disgraceful to freedom; we have reasoned, we have remonstrated with parliament in the most mild and decent language; we have even proceeded to break off our commercial intercourse with our fellow subjects, as the last peaceable admonition that our attachment to no nation on earth should supplant our attachment to liberty. And here we had well hoped was the ultimate step of the controversy. But subsequent events have shewn how vain was even this last remain of confidence in the moderation of the British ministry.[1] During the course of the last year their troops in a hostile manner invested the town of Boston in the province of Massachusets bay, and from that time have held the same beleaguered by sea and land. On the 19th day of April in the present year they made an unprovoked [attack] assault on the inhabitants of the said province at the town of Lexington, murdered eight of them on the spot and wounded many others. From thence

---

[1]Dickinson wrote on margin: "Here insert substance of the Address declaring a Rebellion to exist in Massachusetts Bay."

they proceeded in [the] all the array of war to the town of Concord, where they set upon another party of the inhabitants of the same province, killing many of them also, burning houses, and laying waste property, until repressed by [the arms of[1]] the people[2] suddenly assembled to oppose this cruel aggression. Hostilities thus commenced on the part of the ministerial army have been since by them pursued without regard to faith or to fame. The inhabitants of the town of Boston in order to procure their enlargement having entered into treaty with [a certain Thomas Gage] General Gage their Governor [principal instigator of these enormities[3]] it was stipulated that the said inhabitants,[4] having first deposited their arms with their own magistrates [their arms and military stores] should have free liberty to depart from out of the said town taking with them their other [good and] effects. Their arms [and military stores] they accordingly delivered in, and claimed the stipulated license of departing with their effects. But in open violation of plighted faith and honour, in defiance of the sacred obligations of treaty which even savage nations observe, their arms [and warlike stores,] deposited with their own magistrates to be preserved as their property, were immediately seized by a body of armed men under orders from the said [Thomas Gage] General, the greater part of the inhabitants were detained in the town, and the few permitted to depart were compelled to leave their most valuable effects behind. We leave the world to [their] it's own reflections on this atrocious perfidy. That we might no longer doubt the ultimate aim of these ministerial maneuvres [the same Thomas] General Gage, by proclamation bearing date the 12th day of June, after reciting the grossest falsehoods and calumnies against the good people of these colonies, proceeds to declare them all, either by name or description, to be rebels and traitors, to supersede [by his own authority] the exercise of the common law of the said province, and to proclaim and order instead thereof the use and exercise of the law martial. This bloody edict issued, he has proceeded to commit further ravages and murders in the same province, burning the town of Charlestown, attacking and killing great numbers of the people residing or assembled therein; and is now going on in an avowed course of murder and devastation, taking every occasion to destroy the lives and properties of the inhabitants [of the said province.]

To oppose his arms, we also have taken arms. We should be wanting to ourselves, we should be perfidious to posterity, we should be unworthy that free ancestry from [whom] which we derive our decent, should we submit with folded arms to military butchery and depredation to gratify the lordly ambition, or sate the avarice of a British ministry. We do then most solemnly, before god and the world declare that, regardless of every consequence, at the risk of every distress, the arms we have been compelled

---

[1]Dickinson wrote in the word "country."
[2]"Only" inserted by Dickinson.
[3]Dickinson interlined "to procure their enlargement."
[4]Dickinson inserted "after."

to assume we will [wage] use with perseverance, exerting to their utmost energies all those powers which our creator hath given us, to [guard] preserve that liberty which he committed to us in sacred deposit and to protect from every hostile hand our lives and our properties. But that this [our] declaration may not disquiet the minds of our [good] fellow subjects[1] in *any parts* of the empire,[2] we do further assure them that we mean not in any wise to affect that union with them in which we have so long and so happily lived, and which we wish so much to see again restored That necessity must be hard indeed which may force upon us this desperate measure, or induce us to avail ourselves of any aid [which] their enemies might proffer. We did not embody a soldiery to commit aggression on them; we did not raise armies for glory or for conquest; we did not invade their island carrying death or slavery to it's inhabitants. [We took arms] in defence of our persons and properties under actual violation, [we have taken up arms] we took up arms; when that violence shall be removed, when hostilities shall cease on the part of the aggressors, hostilities shall cease on our part also. [The moment they withdraw their armies, we will disband ours.] For the atchievment of this happy event, we call for and confide in the good offices of our fellow subjects beyond the Atlantic. Of their friendly dispositions we do not yet cease to hope; aware, as they must be, that they have nothing more to expect from the same common enemy, than the humble favour of being last devoured. And we devoutly implore the assistance of Almight god to conduct us happily thro' this great conflict, to dispose the minds of his majesty, his ministers, and parliament to [reasonable terms] reconciliation with us on reasonable terms, and to deliver us from the evils of a civil war.

Q.  If it might not be proper to take notice of Ld. Chatham's Plan and its being refected, mentioning his great abilities.[3]

Q.  If it might not be proper to

## Final Form

A declaration by the Representatives of the United Colonies of North America, now met in General Congress at Philadelphia, setting forth the causes and necessity of their taking up arms.

If it was possible for men, who exercise their reason, to believe, that the Divine Author of our existence intended a part of the human race to hold an absolute property in, and an unbounded power over others, marked out by his infinite goodness and wisdom, as the objects of a legal domination never rightfully resistible, however severe and oppressive, the Inhabitants of these Colonies might at least require from the Parliament of Great Britain some evidence, that this dreadful authority over them, has been granted to that body. But a reverence for our great Creator, principles of humanity, and the dictates of common sense, must convince all those who reflect upon the

---

[1]"Friends and" was suggested by Dickinson.
[2]"In Britain or other," inserted by Dickinson.
[3]This paragraph is in the writing of Dickinson.

subject that government was instituted to promote the welfare of mankind, and ought to be administered for the attainment of that end. The legislature of Great Britain, however, stimulated by an inordinate passion for a power, not only unjustifiable, but which they know to be peculiarly reprobated by the very constitution of that kingdom, and desperate of success in any mode of contest, where regard should be had to truth, law, or right, have at length, deserting those, attempted to effect their cruel and impolitic purpose of enslaving these Colonies by violence, and have thereby rendered it necessary for us to close with their last appeal from Reason to Arms.—Yet, however blinded that Assembly may be, by their intemperate rage for unlimited domination, so to slight justice and the opinion of mankind, we esteem ourselves bound, by obligations of respect to the rest of the world, to make known the justice of our cause.

Our forefathers, inhabitants of the island of Great Britain, left their native land, to seek on these shores a residence for civil and religious freedom. At the expence of their blood, at the hazard of their fortunes, without the least charge to the country from which they removed, by unceasing labor, and an unconquerable spirit, they effected settlements in the distant and inhospitable wilds of America, then filled with numerous and war like nations of barbarians. Societies or governments, vested with perfect legislatures, were formed under charters from the crown, and an harmonious intercourse was established between the colonies and the kingdom from which they derived their origin. The mutual benefits of this union became in a short time so extraordinary, as to excite astonishment. It is universally confessed, that the amazing increase of the wealth, strength, and navigation of the realm, arose from this source; and the minister, who so wisely and successfully directed the measures of Great Britain in the late war, publicly declared, that these colonies enabled her to triumph over her enemies.—Towards the conclusion of that war, it pleased our sovereign to make a change in his counsels.—From that fatal moment, the affairs of the British empire began to fall into confusion, and gradually sliding from the summit of glorious prosperity, to which they had been advanced by the virtues and abilities of one man, are at length distracted by the convulsions, that now shake it to its deepest foundations. The new ministry finding the brave foes of Britain, though frequently defeated, yet still contending, took up the unfortunate idea of granting them a hasty peace, and of then subduing her faithful friends.

These devoted colonies were judged to be in such a state, as to present victories without bloodshed, and all the easy emoluments of statuteable plunder.—The uninterrupted tenor of their peaceable and respectful behaviour from the beginning of colonization, their dutiful, zealous, and useful services during the war, though so recently and amply acknowledged in the most honorable manner by his majesty, by the late king, and by Parliament, could not save them from the meditated innovations.—Parliament was influenced to adopt the pernicious project, and assuming a new power over them, have, in the course of eleven years, given such decisive specimens of the spirit and consequences attending this power, as to leave no doubt concerning the effects of acquiescence under it. They have undertaken to give and grant our money without our consent, though we have ever exercised an exclusive right to dispose of our own property; statutes have been passed for extending the jurisdiction of courts of Admiralty and Vice-Admiralty beyond their ancient limits; for depriving us of the accustomed and inestimable privilege of trial by jury, in cases affecting both life and property; for suspending the legislature of one of the colonies; for interdicting all commerce to the capital of another; and for altering fundamentally the form of government established by charter, and secured by acts colonists from legal trial, and in effect, from punishment; for erecting in a neighboring province, acquired by the joint arms of Great Britain and America, a despotism dangerous to our very existence; and for quartering soldiers upon the colonists in time of profound peace. It has also been resolved in parliament, that colonists charged with committing certain offences, shall be transported to England to be tried.

But why should we enumerate our injuries in detail? By one statute it is declared, that parliament can "of right make laws to bind us IN ALL CASES WHATSOEVER." What is to defend us against so enormous, so unlimited a power? Not a single man of those who assume it, is chosen by us; or is subject to our controul or influence; but, on the contrary, they are all of them exempt from the operation of such laws, and an American revenue, if not diverted from the ostensible purposes for which it is raised, would actually lighten their own burdens in proportion as they increase ours. We saw the misery to which such despotism would reduce us. We for ten years incessantly and ineffectually besieged the Throne as supplicants; we reasoned, we remonstrated with parliament, in the most mild and decent language. But Administration, sensible that we should regard these oppressive measures as freemen ought to do, sent over fleets and armies to enforce them. The indignation of Americans was aroused, it is true; but it was the indignation of a virtuous, loyal, and affectionate people. A Congress of Delegates from the United Colonies was assembled at Philadelphia, on the fifth day of last September. We resolved again to offer an humble and dutiful petition to the King, and also addressed our fellow-subjects of Great Britain. We have pursued every temperate, every respectful measure: we have even proceeded to break off our commercial intercourse with our fellow-subjects, as the last peaceable admonition, that our attachment to no nation upon earth should supplant our attachment to liberty.—This, we flattered ourselves, was the ultimate step of the controversy: But subsequent events have shewn, how vain was this hope of finding moderation in our enemies.

Several threatening expressions against the colonies were inserted in his Majesty's speech; our petition, though we were told it was a decent one, and that his Majesty had been pleased to receive it graciously, and to promise laying it before his Parliament, was huddled into both houses amongst a bundle of American papers, and there neglected. The Lords and Commons in their address, in the month of February, said, that "a rebellion at that time actually existed within the province of Massachusetts bay; and that those concerned in it, had been countenanced and encouraged by unlawful combinations and engagements entered into by his Majesty's subjects in several of the other colonies; and therefore they besought his Majesty, that he would take the most effectual measures to enforce due obedience to the laws and authority of the supreme legislature."—Soon after, the commercial intercourse of whole colonies, with foreign countries, and with each other, was cut off by an act of Parliament; by another, several of them were entirely prohibited from the fisheries in the seas near their coasts, on which they always depended for their sustenance; and large re-inforcements of ships and troops were immediately sent over to General Gage.

Fruitless were all the entreaties, arguments, and eloquence of an illustrious band of the most distinguished Peers, and Commoners, who nobly and strenuously asserted the justice of our cause, to stay, or even to mitigate the heedless fury with which these accumulated and unexampled outrages were hurried on.—Equally fruitless was the interference of the city of London, of Bristol, and many other respectable towns in our favour. Parliament adopted an insidious manoeüvre calculated to divide us, to establish a perpetual auction of taxations where colony should bid against colony, all of them uninformed what ransom would redeem their lives; and thus to extort from us, at the point of the bayonet, the unknown sums that should be sufficient to gratify, if possible to gratify, ministerial rapacity, with the miserable indulgence left to us of raising, in our own mode, the prescribed tribute. What terms more rigid and humiliating could have been dictated by remorseless victors to conquered enemies? In our circumstances to accept them, would be to deserve them.

Soon after the intelligence of these proceedings arrived on this continent, General Gage, who in the course of the last year had taken possession of the town of Boston, in the province of Massachusetts Bay, and still occupied it as a garrison, on the 19th day of April, sent out from that place a large detachment of his army, who made an unprovoked assault on the inhabitants of the said province, at the town of Lexington, as appears by the affidavits of a great number of persons, some of whom were officers and soldiers of that detachment, murdered eight of the inhabitants, and wounded many others. From thence the troops proceeded in warlike array to the town of Concord, where they set upon another party of the inhabitants of the same province, killing several and wounding more, until compelled to retreat by the country people suddenly assembled to repel this cruel aggression. Hostilities, thus commenced by the British troops, have been since prosecuted by them without regard to faith or reputation.—The inhabitants of Boston being confined within that town by the General their Governor, and having, in order to procure their dismission, entered into a treaty with him, it was stipulated that the said inhabitants having deposited their arms with their own magistrates, should have liberty to depart, taking with them their other effects. They accordingly delivered up their arms, but in open violation of honor, in defiance of the obligation of treaties, which even savage nations esteemed sacred, the Governor ordered the arms deposited as aforesaid, that they might be preserved for their owners, to be seized by a body of soldiers; detained the greatest part of the inhabitants in the town, and compelled the few who were permitted to retire, to leave their most valuable effects behind.

By this perfidy wives are separated from their husbands, children from their parents, the aged and the sick from their relations and friends, who wish to attend and comfort them; and those who have been used to live in plenty and even elegance, are reduced to deplorable distress.

The General, further emulating his ministerial masters, by a proclamation bearing date on the 12th day of June, after venting the grossest falsehoods and calumnies against the good people of these colonies, proceeds to "declare them all, either by name or description, to be rebels and traitors, to supersede the course of the common law, and instead thereof to publish and order the use and exercise of the law martial."—His troops have butchered our countrymen, have wantonly burnt Charles-Town, besides a considerable number of houses in other places; our ships and vessels are seized; the necessary supplies of provisions are intercepted, and he is exerting his utmost power to spread destruction and devastation around him.

We have received certain intelligence that General Carleton, the Governor of Canada, is instigating the people of that province and the Indians to fall upon us; and we have but too much reason to apprehend, that schemes have been formed to excite domestic enemies against us. In brief, a part of these colonies now feels, and all of them are sure of feeling, as far as the vengance of administration can inflict them, the complicated calamities of fire, sword, and famine.—We are reduced to the alternative of chusing an unconditional submission to the tyranny of irritated ministers, or resistance by force.—The latter is our choice.—We have counted the cost of this contest, and find nothing so dreadful as voluntary slavery.—Honor, justice, and humanity, forbid us tamely to surrender that freedom which we received from our gallent ancestors, and which our innocent posterity have a right to receive from us. We cannot endure the infamy and guilt of resigning succeeding generations to that wretchedness which enevitably awaits them, if we basely entail hereditary bondage upon them.

Our cause is just. Our union is perfect. On internal resources are great, and, if neccessary, foreign assistance is undoubtedly attainable.—We gratefully acknowledge, as signal instances of the Divine favour towards us, that his Providence would not permit us to be called into this severe controversy, until we were grown up to our present strength, had been previously exercised in warlike operation, and possessed of the means of defending ourselves.—With hearts fortified with these animating reflections, we most solemnly, before God and the world, declare, that, exerting the utmost energy of those powers, which our beneficent Creator hath graciously bestowed upon us, the arms we have been compelled by our enemies to assume, we will, in defiance of every hazard, with unabating firmness and perseverance, employ for the preservation of our liberties; being with our [one] mind resolved to dye Free-men rather than live Slaves.

Lest this declaration should disquiet the minds of our friends and fellow-subjects in any part of the empire, we assure them that we mean not to dissolve that Union which has so long and so happily subsisted between us, and which we sincerely wish to see restored.—Necessity has not yet driven us into that desperate measure, or induced us to excite any other nation to war against them.—We have not raised armies with ambitious designs of separating from Great Britain, and establishing independent states. We fight not for glory or for conquest. We exhibit to mankind the remarkable spectacle of people attacked by unprovoked enemies, without any imputation or even suspicion of offence. They boast of their privileges and civilization, and yet proffer no milder conditions than servitude or death.

In our own native land, in defence of the freedom that is our birth-right, and which we ever enjoyed till the late violation of it—for the protection of our property, acquired solely by the honest industry of our fore-fathers and ourselves, against violence actually offered, we have taken up arms. We shall lay them down when hostilities shall cease on the part of the aggressors, and all danger of their being renewed shall be removed, and not before.

With the humble confidence in the mercies of the supreme and impartial Judge and Ruler of the universe, we most devoutly implore his divine goodness to protect us happily through this great conflict, to dispose our adversaries to reconciliation on reasonable terms, and thereby to relieve the empire from the calamities of civil war.

By order of Congress,

JOHN HANCOCK,

*President.*

Attested,

CHARLES THOMSON,

*Secretary.*

*Philadelphia, July* 6th, 1775.

# 3-a

# John Adams on State Governments

This passage from John Adams's *Autobiography* shows the problem of America's Alternatives as he saw it at the time when the colonies needed guidance about the formation of new governments. The imperative need for such authorities really determined the outcome—and thus placed the conciliationists in a tactically weaker position. But the problem of new governments was inseparable from the problem of the form they were to take. Adams's confidence in the intelligence and political wisdom of the American people gave him a great deal of reassurance, as his entry shows; though it should be added that his own reservations began to develop when he had seen more of their efforts over the following few years.

One point to note here is the persistence of the out-of-date notion that the British administration had a "Scotch faction" at its head. Bute had actually lost all influence more than ten years earlier; Mansfield, who was Lord Chancellor, was no more influential in making policy than Lord North's other ministers. Mansfield, incidentally, had left Scotland as a youth and never returned.

## Document†

Dr. Benjamin Church had brought to Congress a letter from the provincial convention of Massachusetts relative to the question of organizing the state government. The letter is printed in full in the *Journals* under June 2. It is also in Force, *Am. Arch* fourth ser., II. 620; *cf. ibid.*, p. 806. Concerning the proceedings thereon John Adams says in his Autobiography:

"It is necessary that I should be a little more particular, in relating the rise and progress of the new government of the States.

"On Friday, June 2d, 1775,

"The President laid before Congress a letter from the Provincial Convention of Massachusetts Bay, dated May 16th. . . .

"This subject had engaged much of my attention before I left Massachusetts, and had been frequently the subject of conversation between me and many of my friends, Dr. Winthrop, Dr. Cooper, Colonel Otis, the two Warrens, Major Hawley, and others, besides my colleagues in Congress, and lay with great weight upon my mind, as the most difficult and dangerous business that we had to do; (for from the beginning, I always expected we

†From: Edmund C. Burnett, ed., *Letters of Members of The Continental Congress* (Washington, D.C.: The Carnegie Institution, 1921), vol. 1, p. 106.

should have more difficulty and danger, in our attempts to govern ourselves, and in our negotiations and connections with foreign powers, than from all the fleets and armies of Great Britain.) It lay, therefore, with great weight upon my mind, and when this letter was read, I embraced the opportunity to open myself in Congress, and most earnestly to entreat the serious attention of all the members, and of all the continent, to the measures which the times demanded. For my part, I thought there was great wisdom in the adage, 'when the sword is drawn, throw away the scabbard.' Whether we threw it away voluntarily or not, it was useless now, and would be useless forever. The pride of Britain, flushed with late triumphs and conquests, their infinite contempt of all the power of America, with an insolent, arbitrary Scotch faction, with a Bute and Mansfield at their head for a ministry, we might depend upon it, would force us to call forth every energy and resource of the country, to seek the friendship of England's enemies, and we had no rational hope, but from the *Ratio ultima regum et rerumpublicarum*. These efforts could not be made without government, and as I supposed no man would think of consolidating this vast continent under one national government, we should probably, after the example of the Greeks, the Dutch, and the Swiss, form a confederacy of States, each of which must have a separate government. That the case of Massachusetts was the most urgent, but that it could not be long before every other Colony must follow for example. That with a view to this subject, I had looked into the ancient and modern confederacies for examples, but they all appeared to me to have been huddled up in a hurry, by a few chiefs. But we had a people of more intelligence, curiosity, and enterprise, who must be all consulted, and we must realize the theories of the wisest writers, and invite the people to erect the whole building with their own hands, upon the broadest foundation. That this could be done only by conventions of representatives chosen by the people in the several colonies, in the most exact proportions. That it was my opinion that Congress ought now to recommend to the people of every Colony to call such conventions immediately, and set up governments of their own, under their own authority; for the people were the source of all authority and original of all power. These were new, strange, and terrible doctrines to the greatest part of the members, but not a very small number heard them with apparent pleasure, and none more than Mr. John Rutledge, of South Carolina, and Mr. John Sullivan, of New Hampshire."

# 3-b

## Congress's Reply to Lord North's Olive Branch

It appears from Jefferson's *Memoirs* that Franklin, John Adams, Richard Henry Lee, and Jefferson were appointed as a committee to consider and report on Lord North's conciliatory proposition (see Document 2). The Virginia Assembly had already made an answer which was approved by the committee, and the official reply drew substantially on the Virginia document.

This statement finds the Congress in its most constitutionally correct and judicious mood. It is worth noting, however, that in addition to the constitutional objections to the powers to be exercised by Parliament, the committee and through it the Congress pointed out that the colonists could not now be satisfied by an offer of forebearance on the question of taxation. They had other grievances over the "Intolerable" acts and the Quebec Act—which they regarded in the same light—and there was no offer to repeal these.

*Document†*

### MONDAY, JULY 31, 1775

*Report on Lord North's Motion*

The Congress took the said resolution into consideration, and are thereupon, of opinion,

That the colonies of America are entitled to the sole and exclusive privilege of giving and granting their own money: that this involves a right of deliberating whether they will make any gift, for what purposes it shall be made, and what shall be its amount; and that it is a high breach of this privilege for any body of men, extraneous to their constitutions, to prescribe

†From: *Journals of the Continental Congress*, vol. 2, pp. 225-34.

the purposes for which money shall be levied on them, to take to themselves the authority of judging of their conditions, circumstances, and situations, and of determining the amount of the contribution to be levied.

That as the colonies possess a right of appropriating their gifts, so are they entitled at all times to enquire into their application, to see that they be not wasted among the venal and corrupt for the purpose of undermining the civil rights of the givers, nor yet be diverted to the support of standing armies, inconsistent with their freedom and subversive of their quiet. To propose, therefore, as this resolution does, that the monies given by the colonies shall be subject to the disposal of parliament alone, is to propose that they shall relinquish this right of inquiry, and put it in the power of others to render their gifts ruinous, in proportion as they are liberal.

That this privilege of giving or of withholding our monies, is an important barrier against the undue exertion of prerogative, which, if left altogether without controul, may be exercised to our great oppression; and all history shews how efficacious is its intercession for redress of grievances and re-establishment of rights, and how improvident it would be to part with so powerful a mediator.

We are of opinion that the proposition contained in this resolution is unreasonable and insidious: Unreasonable, because, if we declare we accede to it, we declare, without reservation, we will purchase the favor of parliament, not knowing at the same time at what price they will please to estimate their favor; it is insidious, because, individual colonies, having bid and bidden again, till they find the avidity of the seller too great for all their powers to satisfy; are then to return into opposition, divided from their sister colonies whom the minister will hve previously detached by a grant of easier terms, or by an artful procrastination of a definitive answer.

That the suspension of the exercise of their pretended power of taxation being expressly made commensurate with the continuance of our gifts, these must be perpetual to make that so. Whereas no experience has shewn that a gift of perpetual revenue secures a perpetual return of such or of kind disposition. On the contrary, the parliament itself, wisely attentive to this observation, are in the established practice of granting their supplies from year to year only.

Desirous and determined, as we are, to consider, in the most dispassionate view, every seeming advance towards a reconciliation made by the British parliament, let our brethren of Britain reflect, what would have been the sacrifice to men of free spirits, had even fair terms been proffered, as these insidious proposals were with circumstances of insult and defiance. A proposition to give our money, accompanied with large fleets and armies, seems addressed to our fears rather than to our freedom. With what patience would Britons have received articles of treaty from any power on earth when borne on the point of the bayonet by military plenipotentiaries?

We think the attempt unnecessary to raise upon us by force or by threats, our proportional contributions to the common defence, when all know, and themselves acknowledge, we have fully contributed, whenever called upon to do so in the character of freemen.

We are of opinion it is not just that the colonies should be required to oblige themselves to other contributions, while Great Britain possesses a monopoly of their trade. This of itself lays them under heavy contribution. To demand, therefore, additional aids in the form of a tax, is to demand the double of their equal proportion: if we are to contribute equally with the other parts of the empire, let us equally with them enjoy free commerce with the whole world. But while the restrictions on our trade shut to us the resources of wealth, is it just we should bear all other burthens equally with those to whom every resource is open?

We conceive that the British parliament has no right to intermeddle with our provisions for the support of civil government, or administration of justice. The provisions we have made, are such as please ourselves, and are agreeable to our own circumstances: they answer the substantial purposes of government and of justice, and other purposes than these should not be answered. We do not mean that our people shall be burthened with oppressive taxes, to provide sinecures for the idle or the wicked, under colour of providing for a civil list. While parliament pursue their plan of civil government within their own jurisdiction, we also hope to pursue ours without molestation.

We are of opinion the proposition is altogether unsatisfactory, because it imports only a suspension of the mode, not a renunciation of the pretended right to tax us: because, too, it does not propose to repeal the several Acts of Parliament passed for the purposes of restraining the trade, and altering the form of government of one of our colonies: extending the boundaries and changing the government of Quebec; enlarging the jurisdiction of the courts of Admiralty and vice-Admiralty; taking from us the rights of trial by a jury of the vicinage, in cases affecting both life and property; transporting us into other countries to be tried for criminal offences; exempting, by mock-trial, the murderers of colonists from punishment; and quartering soldiers on us in times of profound peace. Nor do they renounce the power of suspending our own legislatures, and of legislating for us themselves in all cases whatsoever. On the contrary, to shew they mean no discontinuance of injury, they pass acts, at the very time of holding out this proposition, for restraining the commerce and fisheries of the provinces of New England, and for interdicting the trade of other colonies with all foreign nations, and with each other. This proves, unequivocally, they mean not to relinquish the exercise of indiscriminate legislation over us.

Upon the whole, this proposition seems to have been held up to the world, to deceive it into a belief that there was nothing in dispute between us but the *mode* of levying taxes; and that the parliament having now been so good as to give up this, the colonies are unreasonable if not perfectly satisfied: Whereas, in truth, our adversaries still claim a right of demanding *ad libitum*, and of taxing us themselves to the full amount of their demand, if we do not comply with it. This leaves us without any thing we can call property. But, what is of more importance, and what in this proposal they keep out of sight, as if no such point was now in contest between us, they claim a right to alter our charters and established laws, and leave us without any security for our lives or liberties. The proposition seems also to have been calculated more particularly to lull into fatal security, our well-affected fellow subjects on the other side the water, till time should be given for the operation of those arms, which a British minister pronounced would instantaneously reduce the "cowardly" sons of America to unreserved submission. But, when the world reflects how inadequate to justice are these vaunted terms; when it attends to the rapid and bold succession of injuries, which, during the course of eleven years, have been aimed at these colonies; when it reviews the pacific and respectful expostulations, which, during that whole time, were the sole arms we opposed to them; when it observes that our complaints were either not heard at all, or were answered with new and accumulated injury; when it recollects that the minister himself, on an early occasion, declared "that he would never treat with America, till he had brought her to his feet," and that an avowed partisan of ministry has more lately denounced against us the dreadful sentence, *"delenda est Carthago;"* that this was done in the presence of a British senate, and being unreproved by them, must be taken to be their own sentiment, (especially as the purpose has already in part been carried into execution, by their treatment of Boston and burning of Charles-Town;) when it considers the great armaments with which they have invaded us, and the circumstances of cruelty with which these have commenced and prosecuted hostilities; when these things, we say, are laid together and attentively considered, can the world be deceived into an opinion that we are unreasonable, or can it hesitate to believe with us, that nothing but our own exertions may defeat the ministerial sentence of death or abject submission.

*By order of the* CONGRESS,
John Hancock,
PRESIDENT
*Philadelphia, July* 31, 1775.

# 3-C

## John Adams on Difficulties in Congress

This letter, one of the many which Adams wrote to keep his Massachusetts friends in touch with developments, gives an insight into his appraisal of the balance of forces. It makes clear how little faith he had in the outcome of the negotiations which the congressional majority hoped to bring about, and from which they hoped for peace.

The "Spirited Manifesto" referred to was the Declaration on Taking Up Arms (see Document 3).

### John Adams to James Warren, July 6, 1775

*Document†*

[P.S.] *Secret and Confidential, as the Saying is.*

The Congress is not yet so much alarmed as it ought to be. There are still hopes, that Ministry and Parliament, will immediately receed as soon as they hear of the Battle of Lexington, the Spirit of New York and Phyladelphia, the Permanency of the Union of the Colonies etc.: I think they are much deceived and that we shall have nothing but Deceit and Hostility, Fire, Famine, Pestilence and Sword from Administration and Parliament. Yet the Colonies like all Bodies of Men must and will have their Way and their Humour, and even their Whims.

These opinions of Some Colonies which are founded I think in their Wishes and passions, their Hopes and Fears, rather than in Reason and Evidence will give a whimsical Cast to the Proceedings of this Congress. You will see a strange Oscillation between love and hatred, between War and Peace—Preparations for War and Negociations for Peace. We must have a Petition to the King and a delicate Proposal of Negociation, etc. This Negociation I dread like Death: But it must be proposed. We cant avoid it. Discord and total Disunion would be the certain Effect of a resolute Refusal to petition and negociate. My Hopes are that Ministry will be afraid of Negociation as well as We and therefore refuse it. If they agree to it, We shall have Occasion for all our Wit Vigilance and Virtue to avoid being deceived, wheedled threatened or bribed out of our Freedom. If we Strenuously insist upon our Liberties, as I hope and am pretty sure We shall however, a Negotiation, if agreed to, will terminate in Nothing. it will effect nothing. We may possibly gain Time and Powder and Arms.

†From: Burnett, ed., *Letters of The Continental Congress*, vol. 1, p. 152.

You will see an Address to the People of G. Britain, another to those of Ireland, and another to Jamaica.

You will also see a Spirited Manifesto. We ought immediately to dissolve all Ministerial Tyrannies, and Custom houses, set up Governments of our own, like that of Connecticutt in all the Colonies, confederate together like an indissoluble Band, for mutual defence, and open our Ports to all Nations immediately. This is the system that your Friend has arrived at promoting from first to last: But the Colonies are not yet ripe for it—a Bill of Attainder, etc., may soon ripen them.

# Negotiations for a French Alliance

The news of the American Prohibitory Act, in mid-February, 1776, helped to clarify the issues. Even though a number of conservative and conciliationist members of the Congress seized on the mention of British commissioners as offering new hopes of peace, the act itself told the Americans that they were in a state of rebellion and would be treated as enemies. The need for a French alliance was becoming not only clear but urgent.

The sense of urgency was accentuated by rumors, possibly induced by the British authorities, that the British administration was contemplating a partition treaty with France and Spain. This would have divided up the North American continent and closed all hope either of expansion or of aid from Europe for the British Americans. It is hard to see how such an arrangement could have served long-term British interests, and in fact the British ministry never took such an idea seriously. Some Americans did. But the instructions to Deane bear no specific sign of this anxiety, as they might have been expected to do; he could, for example, have been told to find out as much as possible about such plans.

Deane received instructions from both the Secret Committee set up in September, 1775 (mainly for supplies) and from the secret Committee of Correspondence, which afterwards took charge of foreign affairs. The latter committee's instructions are reproduced here. They bear evident marks of Benjamin Franklin's knowledge of France and leading French personalities. This was the beginning of a mission of great importance to the history of the American Revolution.

*Document†*

THE COMMITTEE OF SECRET CORRESPONDENCE TO SILAS DEANE.
March 2, 1776.

We, the underwritten, being the Committee of Congress for secret Correspondence, do hereby certify whom it may concern, that the Bearer, the

†From: Burnett, ed., *Letters of the Continental Congress*, vol. 1, pp. 374-73.

Honorable Silas Deane Esquire, one of the Delegates from the Colony of Connecticut, is appointed by us to go into France, there to transact such Business, commercial and political, as we have committed to his Care, in Behalf and by Authority of the Congress of the thirteen united Colonies. In Testimony whereof we have hereunto set our Hands and Seals at Philadelphia, the second Day of March, 1776.

> B. FRANKLIN
> BEN J. HARRISON
> JOHN DICKINSON
> JOHN JAY
> ROBT MORRIS

THE COMMITTEE OF SECRET CORRESPONDENCE TO SILAS DEANE.
PHILADELPHIA March 3, 1776.

On your arrival in France you will, for some time, be engaged in the business of providing goods for the Indian trade. This will give good countenance to your appearing in the character of a merchant, which we wish you continually to retain among the French in general, it being probable that the court of France may not like it should be known publicly that any agent from the Colonies is in that country. When you come to Paris, by delivering Dr. Franklin's letter to Monsieur LeRoy, at the Louvre, and Mr. Dubourg, you will be introduced to a set of acquaintance, all friends to the Americans. By conversing with them you will have a good opportunity of acquiring Parisian French, and you will find in M. Dubourg a man prudent, faithful, secret, intelligent in affairs, and capable of giving you very sage advice.

It is scarce necessary to pretend any other business at Paris than the gratifying of that curiosity, which draws numbers thither yearly, merely to see so famous a city. With the assistance of Monsieur Dubourg, who understands English, you will be able to make immediate application to Monsieur de Vergennes, *ministre des affaires etrangères*, either personally or by letter, if M. Dubourg adopts that method, acquainting him that you are in France upon business of the American Congress, in the character of a merchant, having something to communicate to him that may be mutually beneficial to France and the North American Colonies; that you request an audience of him, and that he would be pleased to appoint the time and place. At this audience, if agreed to, it may be well to show him first your letter of credence, and then acquaint him that the Congress, finding that in the common course of commerce, it was not practicable to furnish the continent of America with the quantity of arms and ammunition necessary for its defense (the ministry of Great Britain having been extremely industrious to prevent it), you have been dispatched by their authority to apply to some European power for a supply. That France had been pitched on for the first application, from an opinion that if we should, as there is a great appearance we shall, come to a total separation from Great Britain, France would be looked upon as the power whose friendship it would be fittest for us to obtain and cultivate. That the commercial advantages Britain had enjoyed with the Colonies had contributed greatly to her late wealth and importance. That it is likely great part of our commerce will naturally fall to the share of France, especially if she favors us in this application, as that will be a means of gaining, and securing the friendship of the Colonies; and that as our trade was rapidly increasing with our increase of people, and, in a greater proportion, her part of it will be extremely valuable. That the supply we at present want is clothing and arms, for twenty-five thousand men, with a suitable quantity of ammunition, and one hundred field pieces. That we mean to pay for the same by remittances to France, or through Spain, Portugal, or the French Islands, as soon as our navigation can be protected by ourselves or friends; and that we, besides, want great quantities of linens and woolens, with other articles for the Indian trade, which you are now actually purchasing, and for which you ask no credit, and that the whole, if France should grant the other supplies, would make a cargo which it might be well to secure by a convoy of two or three ships of war.

If you should find M. de Vergennes reserved, and not inclined to enter into free conversation with you, it may be well to shorten your visit, request him to consider what you have proposed, acquaint him with your place of lodging, that you may yet stay sometime at Paris, and that, knowing how precious his time is, you do not presume to ask another audience; but that, if he should have any commands for you, you will, upon the least notice, immediately wait upon him. If, at a future conference, he should be more free, and you find a disposition to favor the Colonies, it may be proper to acquaint him that they must necessarily be anxious to know the disposition of France on certain points, which, with his permission, you would mention, such as whether, if the Colonies should be forced to form themselves into an independent State, France would probably acknowledge them as such, receive their embassadors, enter into any treaty or alliance with them, for commerce or defense, or both? If so, on what principal conditions? Intimating that you shall speedily have an opportunity of sending to America, if you do not immediately return, and that he may be assured of your fidelity and secrecy in transmitting carefully anything he would wish to convey to the Congress on that subject. In subsequent conversations you may as you find it convenient, enlarge on these topics that have been the subjects of our conferences with you, to which you may occasionally add the well-known substantial answers we usually give to the several calumnies thrown out against us. If these supplies on the credit of the Congress should be refused, you are to endeavor the obtaining a permission of purchasing those articles, or so much of them as you can find credit for. You will keep a daily journal of all your material transactions, and particularly of what passes in your conversation with great personages; and you will, by every safe opportunity, furnish us with such information as may be important. When your business in France admits of it, it may be well to go into Holland, and visit our agent there, M. Dumas, conferring with him on subjects that may promote our interest, and on the means of communication.

You will endeavor to procure a meeting with Mr. Bancroft by writing a letter to him, under cover to Mr. Griffiths, at Turnham Green, near London, and desiring him to come over to you in France or Holland, on the score of old acquaintance. From him you may obtain a good deal of information of what is now going forward in England, and settle a mode of continuing a correspondence. It may be well to remit a small bill to defray his expenses in coming to you, and avoid all political matters in your letter to him. You will also endeavor to correspond with Mr. Arthur Lee, agent of the Colonies in London. You will endeavor to obtain acquaintance with M. Garnier, late *chargé des affaires de France en Angleterre*, if now in France, or, if returned to England, a correspondence with him, as a person extremely intelligent and friendly to our cause. From him you may learn many particulars occasionally, that will be useful to us.

B. FRANKLIN
BENJ. HARRISON
JOHN DICKINSON
ROBERT MORRIS
JOHN JAY

# 5

## Views on Independence

### Letters For and Against Independence Now

These letters have been selected for the light they throw on the extremely different attitudes of influential members of Congress. John Adams as early as March 23 saw positive action as America's only path (*Alternative 3: Resistance for independence*). The letters of Carter Braxton and Edward Rutledge, though written months later, still argued the case for delay. Delay, while the colonists continued to build up their pressure, could still mean ultimate conciliation—or so it was hoped (*Alternative 1-c*). But of course a declaration of independence would close that path forever.

Adams's faith in the power of the colonies as exhibited in his final paragraph, was touching but unrealistic. The colonists had before them a formidable struggle against the power of Britain, which they could not have won without the aid of France. Perhaps Adams's kind of faith was necessary in order to make the venture possible—but he knew better than to suppose for long that America could really stand alone, and soon became one of its ablest representatives in Europe.

### Document[†]

#### JOHN ADAMS TO HORATIO GATES.
PHILADELPHIA March 23, 1776.

*Dear Sir*

. . . . I agree with you, that in Politicks the Middle way is none at all. If we finally fail in this great and glorious Contest, it will be by bewildering ourselves in grouping after this middle way. We have hitherto conducted half a war, acted upon the Line of Defence, etc. etc. But you will see by tomorrow's Paper, that for the future we are likely to wage three Quarters of a war. The Continental ships-of-war, and Provincial ships-of-war, and Letters of Marke and Privateers are permitted to cruise upon British Property, wherever found on the ocean. This is not Independency you know, nothing like it.

If a Post or two more, should bring you unlimited Latitude of Trade to all Nations, and a polite Invitation to all Nations to trade with you, take care

[†]From: Burnett, ed., *Letters of the Continental Congress*, vol. 1, pp. 405-6, 420-21, 517-18.

that you dont call it, or think it Independency. No such Matter. Independency is a Hobgoblin of so frightful Mien, that it would throw a delicate Person into Fits to look it in the Face.

I know not whether you have seen the Act of Parliament call'd the restraining Act, or prohibitory Act, or piratical Act, or plundering Act, or Act of Independency, for by all these titles is it called. I think the most apposite is the Act of independency, for King Lords and Commons have united in sundering this country from that I think forever. It is a compleat Dismemberment of the British Empire. It throws thirteen Colonies out of the Royal Protection, levels all Distinctions, and makes us independent in spight of our supplications and entreaties.

It may be fortunate that the Act of Independency should come from the British Parliament, rather than the American Congress; but it is very odd that Americans should hesitate at accepting such a gift from them. However, my dear friend Gates, all our Misfortunes arise from a single source—the Reluctance of the Southern Colonies to Republican Government. The success of this war depends on a skillful steerage of the political vessel. The Difficulty lies in forming Constitutions for particular Colonies, and a Continental Constitution for the whole, each Colony should establish its own Government, and then a League should be formed, between them all. This can be done only on popular Principles and Maxims which are so abhorrent to the Inclinations of the Barons of the South, and the Proprietary Interests in the Middle Colonies as well as to that avarice of Land, which has made upon this Continent so many votaries to Mammon, that I sometimes dread the Consequences. However Patience, Fortitude, and Perseverance, with the Help of Time will get us over these obstructions.

Thirteen Colonies under such a Form of Government as that of Connecticutt, or one not quite so popular, leagued together in a faithfull Confederacy, might bid Defiance to all the Potentates of Europe if united against them. . . . .

CARTER BRAXTON TO LANDON CARTER.

PHILA. April. 14, 1776.

*Dear Sir,*

. . . . Independency and total seperation from Great Britain are the interesting Subjects of all ranks of men and often agitate our Body. It is in truth a delusive Bait which men inconsiderately catch at, without knowing the hook to which it is affixed. It is an Object to be wished for by every American, when it can be obtained with Safety and Honor. That this is not the moment I will prove by Arguments that to me are decisive, and which exist with certainty. Your refined notion of our publick Honor being engaged to await the terms offered by Commissioners operates strongly with me and many others and makes the first reason I would offer. My next is that America is in too defenceless a State for the declaration, having no Alliance with a naval Power nor as yet any Fleet of consequence of her own to protect that trade which is so essential to the prosecution of the War, without which I know we cannot go on much longer. It is said by the Advocates for

Seperation that France will undoubtedly assist us after we have asserted the
State, and therefore they urge us to make the experiment. Would such a blind
precipitate measure as this be justified by Prudence, first to throw off our
connexion with G. Britain and then give ourselves up to the Arms of France?
Would not the Court so famous for Intrigues and Deception avail herself of
our situation and from it exact much severer terms than if we were to treat
with her (G.B.) before hand and settle the terms of any future Alliance.
Surely she would, but the truth of the matter is, there are some who are
affraid to await the Arrival of Commissioners, lest the dispute should be
accomodated much agt their Will even upon the Admission of our own terms.
For however strange it may appear I am satisfied that the eastern Colonies do
not mean to have a Reconciliation and in this I am justified by publick and
private Reasons. To illustrate my Opinion I will beg leave to mention them.
Two of the New England Colonies enjoy a Government purely democratical
the Nature and Principle of which both civil and religious are so totally
incompatible with Monarchy, that they have ever lived in a restless state
under it. The other two tho' not so popular in their frame bordered so near
upon it that Monarchical Influence hung very heavy on them. The best
opportunity in the World being now offered them to throw off all subjection
and embrace their darling Democracy they are determined to accept it. These
are aided by those of a private Nature, but not less cogent. The Colonies of
Massachusetts, and Connecticut who rule the other two, have Claims on the
Province of Pennsylvania in the whole for near one third of the Land within
their Provincial Bounds and indeed the claim extended to its full extent
comes within four miles of this City. This dispute was carried to the King and
Council, and with them it now lies. The Eastern Colonies unwilling they
should now be the Arbiter have asserted their Claims by force, and have at
this time eight hundred men in arms upon the upper part of this Land called
Wyoming, where they are peaceable at present only through the Influence of
the Congress. Then naturally, there arises a heart burning and jealousy
between these people and they must have two very different Objects in View.
The Province of New York is not without her Fears and apprehensions from
the Temper of her Neighbors, their great swarms and small Territory. Even
Virginia is not free from Claim on Pennsylvania nor Maryland from those on
Virginia. Some of the Delegates from our Colony carry their Ideas of right to
lands so far to the Eastward that the middle Colonies dread their being
swallowed up between the Claims of them and those from the East. And yet
without any Adjustment of those disputes and a variety of other matters,
some are for Lugging us into Independence. But so long as these remain
unsettled and men act upon the Principles they ever have done, you may rely,
no such thing will be generally agreed on. Upon reviewing the secret
movements of Men and things I am convinced the Assertion of Independence
is far off. If it was to be now asserted, the Continent would be torn in pieces
by Intestine Wars and Convulsions. Previous to Independence all disputes
must be healed and Harmony prevail. A grand Continental league must be
formed and a superintending Power also. When these necessary Steps are

taken and I see a Coalition formed sufficient to withstand the Power of Britain, or any other, then am I for an independent State and all its Consequences, as then I think they will produce Happiness to America. It is a true saying of a Wit—We must hang together or separately. I will not beg your pardon for intruding this long letter upon your old Age w$^h$ I judged necessary in my situation and to conclude by assuring you I am with great regard

Your affect Nephew[1]

CARTER BRAXTON

[P.S.] If any of our Newspapers will be agreeable say so in your next.

EDWARD RUTLEDGE TO JOHN JAY.

PHILADA. June 29th, 1776.

*My Dear Jay:*

I write this for the express Purpose of requesting that if possible you will give your Attendance in Congress on Monday next. I know full well that your Presence must be highly useful at New York, but I am sincerely convinced that it will be absolutely necessary in this City during the whole of the ensuing Week. A Declaration of Independence, the Form of a Confederation of these Colonies, and a Scheme for a treaty with foreign Powers will be laid before the House on Monday. Whether we shall be able effectually to oppose the first and infuse Wisdom into the others will depend in a great measure upon the exertions of the honest and sensible part of the Members. I trust you will contribute in a considerable degree to effect the Business and therefore I wish you to be with us. Recollect the manner in which your Colony is at this time represented. Clinton has Abilities but is silent in general and wants (when he does speak) that Influence to which he is intitled. Floyd, Wisner, Lewis and Alsop tho' good men, never quit their chairs. You must know the Importance of these Questions too well not to wish to [be] present whilst they are debating and therefore I shall say no more upon the Subject. I have been much engaged lately upon a plan of a Confederation which Dickenson has drawn, it has the Vice of all his Productions to a considerable Degree; I mean the Vice of Refining too much. Unless it's greatly curtailed it never can pass, as it is to be submitted to Men in the respective Provinces who will not be led or rather driven into Measures which may lay the Foundation of their Ruin. If the Plan now proposed should be adopted nothing less than Ruin to some Colonies will be the Consequence of it. The Idea of destroying all Provincial Distinctions and making every thing of the most minute kind bend to what they call the good of the whole, is in other Terms to say that these Colonies must be subject to the Government to the Eastern Provinces. The Force of their Arms I hold exceeding Cheap, but I confess I dread their overruling Influence in Council. I dread their low Cunning, and those levelling Principles which Men without Character and without Fortune in general possess, which are so captivating to the lower class ot Mankind, and which will occasion such a fluctuation of Property as to introduce the greatest disorder. I am resolved to vest the Congress with no more Power than that is

[1]Carter Braxton was the son of George Braxton and Mary Carter, sister of Col. Landon Carter.

absolutely necessary, and to use a familiar Expression, to keep the Staff in our own Hands; for I am confident if surrendered into the Hands of others a most pernicious use will be made of it. If you can't come let me hear from you by the Return of the Post. Compliments of Livingston and G. Morris.   God bless you.

With Esteem and affection
Yrs,
E. RUTLEDGE.

# 5-a

# The Declaration of Independence: Drafts and Final Form

The process of writing the Declaration of Independence began when on June 10, the Congress formally declared its intentions and appointed a select committee to prepare a draft. The making of the Declaration is briefly described in the text (p. 00). We do not have the space to print the successive drafts, which ought to be studied for an understanding of the political as well as the stylistic considerations that had to be resolved before its adoption. For fuller treatment of these and for comparisons of the drafts the reader is referred to Carl L. Becker, *The Declaration of Independence* (new York; 1922; paperback edition, 1959) and Boyd, ed., *Papers of Jefferson*, (Princeton; 1950), vol. 1, pp. 413-433.

Here we print the familiar final version which closed the road to alternative solutions and committed America to the life of an independent republic (*Alternative 3*). The forms of government that Republic was to take were already under discussion, and were to occupy more years of contention and debate before being settled by the adoption of the United States Constitution.

*Document*[†]

## The unanimous Declaration of the thirteen United States of America

When, in the Course of human events, it becomes necessary for one people to dissolve the political bands which have connected them with another, and

[†]From: *Journals of the Continental Congress*, vol. 5, pp. 510-15.

to assume, among the Powers of the earth, the separate and equal station to which the Laws of Nature and of Nature's God entitle them, a decent respect to the opinions of mankind requires that they should declare the causes which impel them to the separation.

We hold these truths to be self-evident, that all men are created equal, that they are endowed by their Creator with certain unalienable Rights, that among these, are Life, Liberty, and the pursuit of Happiness. That, to secure these rights, Governments are instituted among Men, deriving their just Powers from the consent of the governed. That, whenever any form of Government becomes destructive of these ends, it is the right of the People to alter or to abolish it, and to institute new Government, laying its foundation on such Principles, and organizing its Powers in such form, as to them shall seem most likely to effect their Safety and Happiness. Prudence, indeed, will dictate that Governments long established should not be changed for light and transient causes; and, accordingly, all experience hath shewn, that mankind are more disposed to suffer, while evils are sufferable, than to right themselves by abolishing the forms to which they are accustomed. But, when a long train of abuses and usurpations, pursuing invariably the same Object, evinces a design to reduce them under absolute Despotism, it is their right, it is their duty, to throw off such Government, and to provide new Guards for their future Security. Such has been the patient sufferance of these Colonies; and such is now the necessity which constrains them to alter their former Systems of Government. The history of the present King of Great Britain is a history of repeated injuries and usurpations, all having in direct object the establishment of an absolute Tyranny over these States. To prove this, let Facts be submitted to a candid world.

He has refused his Assent to Laws the most wholesome and necessary for the public good.

He has forbidden his Governors to pass Laws of immediate and pressing importance, unless suspended in their operation till his Assent should be obtained; and when so suspended, he has utterly neglected to attend to them.

He has refused to pass other Laws for the accommodation of large districts of People, unless those People would relinquish the right of Representation in the legislature; a right inestimable to them and formidable to tyrants only.

He has called together legislative bodies at places unusual, uncomfortable, and distant from the depository of their Public Records, for the sole Purpose of fatiguing them into compliance with his measures.

He has dissolved Representative Houses repeatedly, for opposing, with manly firmness, his invasions on the rights of the People.

He has refused for a long time, after such dissolutions, to cause others to be elected; whereby the Legislative Powers, incapable of Annihilation, have returned to the People at large for their exercise; the State remaining in the mean time exposed to all the dangers of invasion from without, and convulsions within.

He has endeavoured to prevent the Population of these States; for that purpose obstructing the Laws for Naturalization of Foreigners; refusing to new Appropriations of Lands.

He has obstructed the Administration of Justice, by refusing his Assent to Laws for establishing Judiciary Powers.

He has made Judges dependent on his Will alone, for the tenure of their offices, and the amount and payment of their salaries.

He has erected a multitude of New Offices, and sent hither swarms of Officers to harrass our People, and eat out their substance.

He has kept among us, in times of Peace, Standing Armies, without the Consent of our legislatures.

He has affected to render the Military independent of and superior to the Civil Power.

He has combined with others to subject us to a jurisdiction foreign to our constitution, and unacknowledged by our laws; giving his Assent to their Acts of pretended Legislation:

For quartering large bodies of armed troops among us:

For protecting them, by a mock Trial, from Punishment for any Murders which they should commit on the Inhabitants of these States:

For cutting off our Trade with all parts of the world:

For imposing Taxes on us without our Consent:

For depriving us, in many cases, of the benefits of Trial by Jury:

For transporting us beyond Seas to be tried to pretended offences:

For abolishing the free System of English Laws in neighbouring province, establishing therein an Arbitrary government, and enlarging its Boundaries, so as to render it at once an example and fit instrument for introducing the same absolute rule into these Colonies:

For taking away our Charters, abolishing our most valuable Laws, and altering fundamentally the Forms of our Governments:

For suspending our own Legislatures, and declaring themselves invested with Power to legislate for us in all cases whatsoever.

He has abdicated Government here, by declaring us out of his protection, and waging War against us.

He plundered our seas, ravaged our Coasts, burnt our towns, and destroyed the Lives of our People.

He is at this time transporting large Armies of foreign Mercenaries to compleat the works of death, desolation and tyranny, already begun with circumstances of Cruelty and perfidy scarcely paralleled in the most barbarous ages, and totally unworthy the Head of a civilized nation.

He has constrained our fellow Citizens, taken Captive on the high Seas, to bear Arms against their Country, to become the executioners of their friends and Brethren, or to fall themselves by their Hands.

He has excited domestic insurrections amongst us, and has endeavoured to bring on the inhabitants of our frontiers, the merciless Indian Savages, whose known rule of warfare, is an undistinguished destruction of all ages, sexes and conditions.

In every stage of these Oppressions, We have Petitioned for Redress, in the most humble terms: Our repeated Petitions, have been answered only by repeated injury. A Prince, whose character is thus marked by every act which may define a Tyrant, is unfit to be the ruler of a free People.

Nor have We been wanting in attentions to our Brittish brethren. We have warned them from time to time of attempts by their legislature to extend an unwarrantable jurisdiction over us. We have reminded them of the circumstances of our emigration and settlement here. We have appealed to their native justice and magnanimity, and we have conjured them by the ties of our common kindred, to disavow these usurpations, which, would inevitably interrupt our connexions and correspondence. They too have been deaf to the voice of justice and of consanguinity. We must, therefore, acquiesce in the necessity, which denounces our Separation, and hold them, as we hold the rest of mankind, Enemies in War, in Peace Friends.

We, therefore, the Representatives of the United States of America, in GENERAL CONGRESS assembled, appealing to the Supreme Judge of the World for the rectitude of our intentions, DO, in the Name, and by Authority of the good People of these Colonies, solemnly PUBLISH and DECLARE, That these United Colonies are, and of Right, ought to be free and Independent States; that they are Absolved from all Allegiance to the British Crown, and that all political connexion between them and the State of Great Britain, is and ought to be totally dissolved; and that, as FREE and INDEPENDENT STATES, they have full Power to levy War, conclude Peace, contract Alliances, establish Commerce, and to do all other Acts and Things which INDEPENDENT STATES may of right do. AND for the support of this Declaration, with a firm reliance on the protection of divine Providence, we mutually pledge to each other our Lives, our Fortunes, and our sacred Honour.

‖ The foregoing declaration was, by order of Congress, engrossed, and signed by the following members: ‖1

*John Hancock.*

JOSIAH BARTLETT.
Wm WHIPPLE.
SAML ADAMS.
JOHN ADAMS.
ROBT TREAT PAINE.
ELBRIDGE GERRY.
STEPH. HOPKINS.
WILLIAM ELLERY.
ROGER SHERMAN.
SAMEL HUNTINGTON.
Wm WILLIAMS.
OLIVER WOLCOTT.
MATTHEW THORNTON.
Wm FLOYD.
PHIL LIVINGSTON.
FRANS LEWIS.

GEO. TAYLOR.
JAMES WILSON.
GEO. ROSS.
CAESAR RODNEY.
GEO READ.
THOS M:KEAN
SAMUEL CHASE.
Wm PACA.
THOS STONE.
CHARLES CARROLL of
    Carrollton.
GEORGE WYTHE.
RICHARD HENRY LEE.
TH. JEFFERSON.
BENJA HARRISON.
THOS NELSON, Jr.

LEWIS MORRIS.

RICH<sup>D</sup> STOCKTON.

JNO WITHERSPOON.

FRA<sup>S</sup> HOPKINSON.

JOHN HART.

ABRA CLARK.

ROB<sup>T</sup> MORRIS.

BENJAMIN RUSH.

BENJ<sup>A</sup> FRANKLIN.

JOHN MORTON.

GEO CLYMER..

JA<sup>S</sup> SMITH.

FRANCIS LIGHTFOOT LEE.

CARTER BRAXTON.

W<sup>M</sup> HOOPER.

JOSEPH HEWES.

JOHN PENN.

EDWARD RUTLEDGE.

THO<sup>S</sup> HEYWARD, Jun<sup>r</sup>.

THOMAS LYNCH, Jun<sup>r</sup>.

ARTHUR MIDDLETON.

BUTTON GWINNETT.

LYMAN HALL.

GEO WALTON..

[1]The text used is that of the engrossed original in the Department of State.

# 5-b

# New York Acts for Independence

It may seem odd that the last document should be subsequent to the Declaration of Independence. But New York's delegates to the Continental Congress could not sign the Declaration until this authority had reached them from their own Provincial Convention in White Plains. The language of that convention stands in striking contrast to that adopted by Congress. Separation has become a "cruel necessity." Until the last moment of the previous convention, many had hoped that this fatal contingency could be averted. Now it was accepted, as a necessity, and without enthusiasm. However, the statement makes a useful point: even those who had hoped for the success of the alternative of conciliation now saw that road as closed. The alternative taken, that of independence, was no longer the choice of the hot-headed enthusiasts or radicals alone, but of all those colonial leaders for whom the defense of their liberties was—and always had been—more important than their allegiance to Britain.

*Document†*

IN CONVENTION OF THE REPRESENTATIVES
"OF THE STATE OF NEW YORK,
*"White Plains, July 9, 1776.*

"*Resolved unanimously,* That the reasons assigned by the Continental Congress for declaring the United Colonies Free and Independent States, are cogent and conclusive; and, that while we lament the cruel necessity which has rendered that measure unavoidable, we approve the same, and will, at the risque of our lives and fortunes, join with the other colonies in supporting it.

"*Resolved,* That a copy of the said declaration and the aforegoing resolution be sent to the chairman of the committee of the county of Westchester with orders to publish the same with beat of Drum, at this place, on Thursday next, and to give directions, that it be published with all

†From: *Journals of the Continental Congress*, vol. 5, p. 560.

convenient speed in the several districts of the county; that copies also be sent to the chairman of the several counties within the state of New York with orders to cause the same to be published in the several districts of their respective counties.

"*Resolved unanimously*, That the delegates of this state, in the Continental Congress, be, and they hereby are authorized to concert and adopt all such measures as they may deem conducive to the happiness and welfare of the United States of America.

"Extract from the minutes,

"ROBERT BENSON, *Secretary.*

# part three

## Bibliographic and Historiographical Essay

This is not intended as a finding list for source materials of the period. However, the high standards of editorship which have developed in recent years, and particularly from the work of Julian P. Boyd, should be mentioned because they have led to actual advances in knowledge. By setting documents in their contexts, explaining references and discussing difficulties of exegesis, the editorial enterprises of Boyd, Butterfield and others have helped to elucidate the course of events. Burnett's collection of *Letters* made a profound difference to the problem of seeing the period as a whole.

The documentary history of individual colonies must be traced in the statutes and constitutional records of each state; all official American constitutional documents to the date of publication were collected by F. N. Thorpe, *Federal and State Constitutions, Colonial Charters and Other Organic Laws,* 7 vols., (Washington, D.C., 1909). For the Congress, a former outline of events, omitting much that would have been of interest, is provided by the *Journals of the Continental Congress,* ed. W. C. Ford, 34 vols. (Washington, D.C., 1904-1937). These journals were edited from previously unpublished records in the Library of Congress as well as from the limited *Journal* as printed from the records made by Charles Thomson, the clerk to the Congress. Ford's *Journals* contain important information such as the record of Galloway's Plan which had previously been omitted, or suppressed.

For leading individuals: Julian P. Boyd, ed., *The Papers of Thomas Jefferson* (Princeton, 1950) vol. 1; L. H. Butterfield, ed., *The Adams Papers,* vol. 2; *Diary 1771-1781* (Cambridge, Mass., 1961); Edmund C. Burnett, ed., *Letters of Members of the Continental Congress* (Washington, D.C., 1921), vol. 1; Robert Green McCloskey, ed., *The Works of James Wilson* (Cambridge, Mass., 1967) vol. 1; William T. Hutchinson and William M. E. Rachal, eds., *The Papers of James Madison* (Chicago, 1962) vol. 1; and W. C. Ford, ed., *Writings of George Washington* (Washington, D.C., 1931-1932) vols. 3-5.

The earliest historians of the movement that culminated in American independence were contemporaries, who had themselves been committed to the struggle. They were witnesses as well as judges of the events. Their evidence as witnesses was frequently influenced and sometimes dominated by their point of view; they had no thought of history as a science of observation but were positively engaged in writing it as a continuation of the action. This does not invalidate their accounts. The point of view is generally clear and explicit, and the evidence they give is often genuine contemporary evidence. When using their work, it is of course necessary to be on one's guard, but that does not present any real difficulties.

On the Whig or patriotic side, the first to deal with the subject as a whole was the Rev. William Gordon, *The History of the Rise, Progress, and Establishment, of the Independence of the United States of America,* 4 vols., (London, 1788, New York, 1789). Almost at the same time came Dr. David Ramsay, the South Carolina physician, with his *History of the American Revolution,* 2 vols., (Philadelphia, 1789). Another early contributor was Charles Stedman, *History of the Origin, Progress, and Termination of the American War,* 2 vols., (Dublin, 1794); followed by the Massachusetts-based Mercy Otis Warren's *History of the Rise, Progress, and Termination of the American Revolution,* 3 vols., (Boston, 1805). Alternative views also became available. Thomas Hutchinson's *The History of the Colony and Province of Massachusetts-Bay* (Boston, 1764 and 1828) has been edited in three volumes by L. S. Mayo, (Cambridge, Mass., 1936). The third volume gives an unflattering account of the leaders of the Revolution in Massachusetts and the mobs who followed them. Peter Oliver, Tory member of the Governor's Council in the same province, wrote a bitter account of the same events from a very personal experience of them, edited by Douglass Adair and John A. Schutz as *Peter Oliver's Origin and Progress of the American Rebellion* (San

Marino, Calif., 1961). Another important Loyalist view came from the exiled Joseph Galloway, *Historical and Political Reflections on the Rise and Progress of the American Rebellion* (London, 1780).

## Military and Diplomatic Histories

This group of studies is generally more technical. The writers are interested in the problems facing either side in the revolutionary situation, rather than in establishing that one side was right (though that point tends to be taken very much for granted in most American studies.) For diplomacy: Samuel Flagg Bemis, *The Diplomacy of the American Revolution* (New York and London, 1935). Military aspects are described in: Justin H. Smith, *Arnold's March from Cambridge to Quebec* (New York and London, 1903); F. W. Coburn, *Battle of April 19, 1775* (Lexington, 1912); Harold Murdock, *The Nineteenth of April, 1775* (Boston, 1923); Howard W. Peckham, *The War for Independence: a Military History* (Chicago, 1958); W. M. Wallace, *Appeal to Arms; a Military History of the Revolution* (New York, 1951); Christopher Ward, *The War of the Revolution*, ed. T. R. Alden (New York, 1952). A clear and professional military history is R. E. DuPuy and T. N. Dupuy, *Compact History of the Revolutionary War* (New York, 1963). The British side is handled with great competence in Piers Mackesy, *The War for America, 1775-1783* (London, 1964). See, also, the general histories listed below, which describe the military aspects; and also the biographies of military men, notably George Washington.

## General Histories of the Origins and Course of the Revolution which Include Discussion of the Events of 1774-1776 in Some Detail

George Bancroft, the Jacksonian politician and diplomatist, extended the English "Whig" tradition of historical writing into an American "democratic" tradition with his *History of the United States from the Discovery of the American Continent*, 10 vols., in several editions (Boston, 1836-1894). Bancroft wrote in the classical style with a sense of drama and a clearer sense of who was right and who was wrong than later and more analytical historians. His account of events leading to independence has necessarily been superseded by the publication of much documentary material, but the outlines remain clear and firm. Richard Hildreth's *History of the United States*, 6 vols., (1849-1856) was the first significant nineteenth-century history to take a skeptical view of the motives of some of the American patriots. Since all general histories contain some account of the onset of independence, they will not be listed here. Late in the nineteenth century the English historian Sir George Otto Trevelyan revived the Whig approach with his finely written *The American Revolution*, 6 vols., (London, 1899-1914); in the same period, Americans began to examine the problems of the revolution with eyes wider open for the possibilities of social conflict and a multiplicity of interests on the American side than the classical Whig tradition had been ready to admit. It would not be strictly correct to describe the history written in the twentieth century as "scientific" in contradistinction to its predecessors; but the recognition of complexities not fully appreciated before brought with it the need for some understanding of different points of view and a somewhat more critical approach to conflicts in the evidence. It was the lack of this approach among Hildreth's contemporaries in the nineteenth century that had led to his work's being largely ignored. Sidney George Fisher was one of the earliest historians to bring a lively sense of reality and a wealth of original research to the subject in *The True History of the American*

*Revolution* (Philadelphia, 1902) and *The Struggle for American Independence*, 2 vols., (Philadelphia, 1908); also C. H. Van Tyne, *The Causes of the War of Independence* (Boston, 1922) treated the issues as arising from conflicts in which American ideas and interests were inherent in British politics and traditions. Meanwhile, interest in the social aspects of historical development gave rise to an ambitious new series, *A History of American Life*, edited by Arthur M. Schlesinger and Dixon Ryan Fox, to which Evarts Boutell Greene contributed *The Revolutionary Generation* (New York, 1943). John C. Miller's two works, *Origins of the American Revolution* (Boston, 1943; rev. ed., Stanford, 1967) and *Triumph of Freedom, 1775-1783* (Boston, 1948) brought a new wealth of documentary analysis to the subject—without departing from a substantially "Whig" line of interpretation. The British scholar Eric Robson's *The American Revolution in its Political and Military Aspects, 1763-1783* (London, 1955) continued the advance in scholarship and in the sophistication of approach. Edmund C. Burnett, *The Continental Congress* (New York, 1941) tells the story as a whole from the formation of the Congress. Other works interpreting the events leading to independence have included J. R. Alden, *The American Revolution, 1775-1783* (New York, 1954); Herbert Aptheker, *The American Revolution 1763-1783* (London, 1960); and Richard B. Morris, *The American Revolution Reconsidered* (New York, 1967); in Jack P. Greene, ed., *The Reinterpretation of the American Revolution, 1763-1789* (New York, 1968), many excellent essays are brought conveniently together. The American crisis presented a continuing problem for British politicians and publicists, whose pronouncements are to be found in a useful volume, Max Beloff, ed., *The Debate on the American Revolution* (London, 1949; 2nd ed., 1960).

## Social Conflict and Special Interests

Since the influence of Marxist views began to take effect in the early twentieth century, American historical writing has recognized social or class conflict as positive ingredients of the processes making for revolution in America. These views were absorbed in the United States in a highly diluted form, however. The earlier manifestations of the new approach, which sought to find social conflict behind the forms of American institutions, came in revisionist views of the Constitution. But the idea of internal conflict behind the movement for Independence was put forward in certain special studies, an early and still classic example being Carl L. Becker's *History of Political Parties in the Province of New York, 1760-1776* (Madison, Wisc., 1909). This remains a fundamental work, which has been touched up but never superseded. The theme is pursued in a fine and carefully researched monograph, Alfred F. Young, *The Democratic Republicans of New York: The Origins, 1763-1797* (Chapel Hill, 1967); Bernard Mason, *The Road to Independence: The Revolutionary Movement in New York, 1773-1777* (Lexington, Ky., 1966) adds information in detail but fails to displace Becker. One of the advances made by this school arose from a realistic recognition that Americans became "Whigs" or patriots because they had material interests in the social and economic order that seemed to be threatened by British policy. The types of interest of course varied very widely, and have been studied in a correspondingly wide variety of monographs. One of the earliest and most influential was Arthur M. Schlesinger, *Colonial Merchants and the American Revolution, 1763-1776* (New York, 1918); see also Charles M. Andrews, *The Boston Merchants and the Non-Importation Movement* (Cambridge, Massachusetts, 1917), and Virginia Harrington, *The New York Merchant on the Eve of the Revolution*

(New York, 1935). General Studies recognizing this dimension of social analysis include: Allan Nevins, *The American States During and After the Revolution* (New York, 1924); T. P. Abernethy, *Western Lands and the American Revolution* (New York, 1937); Merrill Jensen, *The Articles of Confederation* (Madison, Wisc., 1940) and his balanced and thorough work, *The Founding of a Nation: A History of the American Revolution, 1763-1776* (New York, 1968). See also R. R. Palmer, *The Age of the Democratic Revolution* (Princeton, 1959), vol. 1, *The Challenge,* for an interpretation emphasizing political divisions in a wider setting. The growing unity of the urban situation and its peculiar contributions are brought to light in the works of Carl Bridenbaugh, notably *Cities in Revolt: Urban Life in America, 1743-1776* (New York, 1955, reprint ed., 1968) and in his and Jessica Bridenbaugh's *Rebels and Gentlemen: Philadelphia in the Age of Franklin* (New York, 1942). The significant role of the British army not only in disciplining Boston but in tempting it away from its radical posture is the theme of John Shy, *Toward Lexington: The Role of the British Army in the Coming of the American Revolution* (Princeton, 1965). A theme of central importance, never previously put in the centre, is clearly expounded in E. James Ferguson, *The Power of the Purse: A History of American Public Finance, 1776-1790* (Chapel Hill, 1961). For the Black contribution, not uncharacteristically neglected by white historians, see Benjamin Quarles, *The Negro in the American Revolution* (Chapel Hill, 1961). For conflicts of loyalty see William Allen Benton, *Whig Loyalism* (Rutherford, 1969), and Mary Beth Norton, *The British-Americans: The Loyalist Exiles in England* (Boston, 1972). The Anglo-American context of the revolutionary movement is particularly well done in Pauline Maier, *From Resistance to Revolution: Colonial Radicals and the Development of American Opposition to Britain, 1763-1776* (New York, 1972); Bernard Donoughue has studied *British Politics and the American Revolution: The Path to War, 1773-1775* (London, 1964). Recent contributions to the discussion of social and economic conflict are, Richard B. Morris, "Class Struggle and the American Revolution", *William and Mary Quarterly* 19, third ser., (1962); and Marc Egnal and Joseph A. Ernst, "An Economic Interpretation of the American Revolution", *William and Mary Quarterly* 29, third ser., (1972).

## Regional State and Local Studies

There is a long tradition of local history, approached mainly either as state history or as the study of specific cities and their localities. But in more recent years, the intensification of specialist work has led historians into close investigations of local records, which have often yielded rich rewards. Moreover, the impetus given by the "realistic" concern with social conflict and economic interests has usually taken historians further into state or local history. This section is therefore very largely a continuation of the last—which has already included a number of local items. But it also includes several more broadly based general state or local studies—usually of somewhat earlier date. Reading from North to South, the onset of independence provides thematic material for these works. Chilton Williamson, *Vermont in Quandary* (Montpelier, 1949); Richard F. Upton, *Revolutionary New Hampshire* (Hanover, 1936); J. S. Barry, *History of Massachusetts, 1492-1820,* 3 vols., (Boston, 1855-1857); Oscar and Mary F. Handlin, "Radicals and Conservatives in Massachusetts", *New England Quarterly* 17 (1944), and *Commonwealth: Massachusetts 1774-1861* (New York, 1947); Robert J. Taylor, *Western Massachusetts in the Revolution* (Providence, 1954); Robert E. Brown, *Middle-Class Democracy and the Revolution in Massachusetts, 1691-1780* (Ithaca, New York, 1955); this work emphasizes consensus, not conflict. Richard Purcell, *Connecticut in Transition* (Washington, 1918); Oscar Zeichner, *Connecticut's Years of Controversy* (Chapel Hill, 1949); David S. Lovejoy, *Rhode Island Politics and the American Revolution* (Providence, 1958); Benjamin Labaree, *Patriots and Partisans: the Merchants of Newburyport, 1764-1815* (Cambridge, Massachusetts, 1962), and *The Boston Tea Party* (New York, 1964). On New York: Wilbur C. Abbot, *New York in the American Revolution* (New York, 1929); Oscar Theodore Barck, Jr., *New York City During the War for Independence* (New York, 1931); T. J. Wertenbaker, *Father Knickerbocker Rebels* (New York, 1948). Staughton Lynd, "Who Should Rule at Home? Dutchess County, New York, in the American Revolution", *William and Mary Quarterly* 18, third ser., (1961), reopened the argument of Becker; see also, Roger J. Champagne, "New York's Radicals and the Coming of Independence", *Journal of American History* 51 (1964); and Alfred F. Young, above. Also, Bernard Friedman, "The Shaping of the Radical Consciousness of Provincial New York", *Journal of American History* 56 (1970). Much less work has been done on New Jersey, but see Leonard Lundin, *Cockpit of the Revolution: The War for Independence in New Jersey* (New York, 1942). Studies of Pennsylvania politics have had to concern themselves with the complexities of the struggle between Quaker and Proprietary parties as well as the emergence of a genuine radical movement. The process began early, with Charles H. Lincoln, *The Revolutionary Movement in Pennsylvania, 1760-1776* (Philadelphia, 1901); later came J. Paul Selsam, *The Pennsylvania Constitution of 1776: A Study in Revolutionary Democracy* (Philadelphia, 1936), and Theodore Thayer, *Pennsylvania Politics and the Growth of Democracy, 1740-1776* (Harrisburg, 1953). David Hawke, *In the Midst of a Revolution* (Philadelphia, 1961) is particularly central to the problems posed in this book. See also David Jacobson, *John Dickinson and the Revolution in Pennsylvania, 1764-1776* (Berkeley, 1965); and Charles S. Olton, "Philadelphia's Mechanics in the First Decade of the Revolution, 1765-1775", *Journal of American History* 58 (1972). John A. Monroe, *Federalist Delaware, 1775-1815* (New Brunswick, 1954) covers a rather neglected state. Maryland has also had rather scanty attention, despite the excellent introduction provided by Charles A. Barker's *Background to the Revolution in Maryland* (New Haven, 1940). Philip A. Crowl, *Maryland During and After the Revolution* (Baltimore, 1943) is a good monograph; see, further, David Curtis Skaggs, "Maryland's Impulse Toward Social Revolution, 1750-1776", *Journal of American History* 54 (1968). A general treatment of the southern colonies is J. R. Alden, *The South in the Revolution, 1763-1789* (Baton Rouge, 1957). H. J. Eckenrode, *The Revolution in Virginia* (Boston, 1916) remains a standard work; for a valuable regional study, see Freeman H. Hart, *The Valley of Virginia in the American Revolution, 1763-1789* (Chapel Hill, 1942); see also Thad W. Tate, "The Coming of the Revolution in Virginia: Britain's Challenge to Virginia's Ruling Class, 1763-1776", *William and Mary Quarterly* 29, third ser., (1962). For North Carolina it remains necessary to turn to S. A. Ashe, *History of North Carolina*, 2 vols., (Greensboro, 1908-1925); Enoch W. Sikes has traced the *Transition of North Carolina from Colony to Commonwealth* (Baltimore, 1898). For South Carolina, Edward McCrady, *The History of South Carolina in the Revolution, 1775-1780* (New York and London, 1901). For Georgia, see M. L. Daniel, *The Revolutionary Movement in Georgia, 1763-1777* (Chicago, 1937), and Kenneth Coleman, *The American Revolution in Georgia* (Athens, Ga., 1958); P. S. Flippin, "Royal Government in Georgia 1752-1780", *Georgia Historical Quarterly*, 8 (1924), and 13 (1929), bears on the subject from the point of view of the authorities. There are other books and articles dealing with issues touching on the development of attitudes to independence, but this survey suggests that in certain areas the field is less thickly planted than one might have expected.

## Studies Emphasizing the Development of Constitutional and Political Ideas

Lord Acton, "Political Causes of the American Revolution", in *Essays on Church and State by Lord Acton* ed. Douglass Woodruff (New York, 1953); Charles F. Mullett, *Colonial Claims to Home Rule, 1764-75* (Columbia, Mo., 1927), and *Fundamental Law and the American Revolution* (New York, 1933); Randolph G. Adams, *Political Ideas of the American Revolution* (Durham, N. C., 1923); Julian P. Boyd, *Anglo-American Union: Joseph Galloway's Plans* . . . (Philadelphia, 1941); Carl L. Becker, *The Declaration of Independence: A Study in the History of Political Ideas* (New York, 1922) is a literary, textual, and philosophical analysis. Charles H. McIlwain, *The American Revolution: A Constitutional Interpretation* (New York, 1923) and Robert L. Schuyler, *Parliament and the British Empire* (New York, 1929) form a historic controversy. Daniel J. Boorstin, *The Genius of American Politics* (Chicago, 1953) builds a political science edifice on the attitudes attributed to the makers of American institutions in our period. Bernard Bailyn, *Ideological Origins of the American Revolution* (Cambridge, Mass., 1967) has transformed the study of these formative ideas; see also Cecelia M. Kenyon, "Republicanism and Radicalism in the American Revolution: An Old-Fashioned Interpretation", *William and Mary Quarterly* 11, third ser., (1962). For connections between political thought and action see also J. R. Pole, *Political Representation in England and the Origins of the American Republic* (New York and London, 1966; rev. ed., Berkeley, 1971). These works should serve as a reminder that ideas and beliefs are also realities. That view also informs Gordon S. Wood, *The Creation of the American Republic* (Chapel Hill, 1968).

## The Movement Toward Independence

While all general works on the revolution give accounts of the events from 1774 to 1776, and the works so far mentioned help to establish the background of those events, our immediate theme has itself attracted attention over a long period. Some of these studies arise from specific problems in the meaning or identification of documents; others offer explanations of the measures of the Continental Congress. Edmund C. Burnett, *The Continental Congress* (see above) should be mentioned first because his editorship of the *Letters of the Continental Congress* gave him access to much previously uncollected information. But special studies of the Declaration of Independence began much earlier; see Herbert Friedenwald, *The Declaration of Independence, an Interpretation and an Analysis* (New York, 1904); J. H. Hazleton, *The Declaration of Independence* (New York, 1906); Carl L. Becker, *The Eve of Revolution: A Chronicle of the Breach with England* (New York, 1921). We have in some ways been anticipated also by W. A. Brown, *Empire or Independence, a Study in the Failure of Reconciliation, 1774-1783* (Baton Rouge, L.A., 1941) and by Lynn Montross, *The Reluctant Rebels: The Study of the Continental Congress, 1774-1789* (New York, 1950). See also, David Hawke, *A Transaction of Free Men: the Birth and Course of the Declaration of Independence* (New York, 1964); and Merrill Jensen, "The American People and the American Revolution", *Journal of American History* 57 (1970). Textual problems have been pursued in Curtis P. Nettels, "A Link in the Chain of Events Leading to American Independence", *William and Mary Quarterly* 3, third ser. (1946); Julian P. Boyd, *The Declaration of Independence: The Evolution of the*

*Text...* (Princeton, 1945), and "The Authorship of the Declaration of Causes", *Pennsylvania Magazine of History and Biography* 74 (1950); Wilbur Samuel Howell, "The Declaration of Independence and Eighteenth Century Logic", *William and Mary Quarterly* 18, third ser., (1961); Earl Latham, ed., *The Declaration of Independence and the Constitution* (Boston, 1949; rev. ed., 1956); Arthur M. Schlesinger, "The Lost Meaning of 'The Pursuit of Happiness' ", *William and Mary Quarterly* 21, third ser., (1964); Edwin Wolf, "The Authorship of the 1774 Address to the King Restudied," *William and Mary Quarterly* 22, third ser., (1965); and for the question of timing, see James H. Hutson, "The Partition Treaty and the Declaration of American Independence", *Journal of American History* 58 (1972).

## Biographical Studies

Much of our information about political developments has come through the study of individual lives. A limitation of this type of source, of course, is that different persons have lieft very differing amounts and kinds of traces behind them, and the imbalance between Samuel and John Adams in this respect has been mentioned in the text. The following works, ranging from Wirt's *Patrick Henry*, for which the author was able to question some of Henry's contemporaries, down to modern works using materials unknown to earlier biographers, have all contributed to our knowledge of the events leading to independence. Listed alphabetically by subject of biography:

Louise B. Dunbar, "The Royal Governors in the Middle and Southern Colonies on the Eve of the Revolution: A Study in Imperial Personnel," *The Era of the American Revolution* ed. Richard B. Morris *New York, 1939, reprint ed., 1965.*

Charles C. Jones, Jr., *Biographical Sketches of the Delegates of Georgia to the Continental Congress.* Boston, 1891.

Gilbert Chinard, *Honest John Adams.* Boston, 1933.

Page Smith, *John Adams.* 2 vols. New York, 1962.

W. V. Wells, *Life and Public Services of Samuel Adams,* 3 vols. Boston, 1865.

Ralph V. Harlow, *Samuel Adams, Promoter of the Revolution: A Study in Psychology and Politics.* New York, 1923.

John C. Miller, *Sam Adams: Pioneer in Propaganda.* Boston, 1935.

Kate Mason Rowland, *Life of Charles Carroll.* Putnam, 1898.

Ellen Hunt Smith, *Charles Carroll of Carrollton.* Cambridge, Mass., 1945.

Edward P. Alexander, *A Revolutionary Conservative—James Duane of New York.* New York, 1938.

Verner W. Crane, *Benjamin Franklin, Englishman and American.* Baltimore, 1936.

Carl Van Doren, *Benjamin Franklin.* New York, 1938.

Esmond Wright, *Benjamin Franklin and American Independence.* London, 1966.

J. R. Alden, *General Gage in America.* Baton Rouge, 1948.

William Wirt, *Sketches of the Life of Patrick Henry.* Philadelphia, *1818.*

Moses Coit Tyler, *Patrick Henry.* Boston, 1887.

W. W. Henry, *Patrick Henry,* 3 vols. New York, 1891.

George Morgan, *The True Patrick Henry.* Philadelphia and London, 1907.

Robert D. Meade, *Patrick Henry,* 2 vols. Philadelphia and New York, 1957-69.

J. K. Hosmer, *Life of Thomas Hutchinson.* Boston, 1896.

Dumas Malone, *Jefferson the Virginian.* Boston, 1948.

D. D. Wallace, *Life of Henry Laurens.* New York, 1915.

Oliver Perry Chitwood, *Richard Henry Lee.* Morgantown, 1967.

George Dangerfield, *Chancellor Robert R. Livingston of New York, 1746-1813*. New York, 1960.

Irving Brant, *James Madison, the Virginia Revolutionist*. Indianapolis, 1941.

Kate Mason Rowland, *The Life of George Mason, 1725-1792*, 2 vols. New York, 1892.

Helen Hill, *George Mason*. Cambridge, Mass., 1938.

Kenneth R. Rossman, *Thomas Mifflin and the Politics of the American Revolution*. Chapel Hill, 1952.

Daniel Walther, *Gouverneur Morris*. New York, 1934.

Ellis P. Oberholtzer, *Robert Morris, Patriot and Financier*. New York, 1903.

Clarence L. Ver Steeg, *Robert Morris: Revolutionary Financier*. Philadelphia, 1954.

William Tudor, *Life of James Otis of Massachusetts*. Boston, 1923.

M. D. Conway, *The Life of Thomas Paine*, 2 vols. New York, 1892.

Alfred Owen Aldridge, *Man of Reason*. Philadelphia, 1959.

David J. Mays, *Edmund Pendleton*, 2 vols. Cambridge, Mass., 1952.

Benson J. Lossing, *Life and Times of Philip Schuyler*, 2 vols. New York, 1872.

D. R. Gerlach, *Philip Schuyler and the American Revolution*. Lincoln, 1964.

Roger Sherman Boardman, *Roger Sherman*. Philadelphia, 1938.

Lewis R. Harley, *The Life of Charles Thomson*. Philadelphia, 1900.

John Marshall, *Life of George Washington*, 6 vols. Philadelphia, 1805-1807.

Bernard Knollenberg, *Washington and the Revolution*. New York, 1940.

D. S. Freeman, *George Washington*, 6 vols. New York, 1948-54.

Curtis P. Nettels, *George Washington and American Independence*. Boston, 1951.

Lawrence S. Mayo, *John Wentworth, Governor of New Hampshire*. Cambridge, Mass., 1921.

Page Smith, *James Wilson*. Chapel Hill, 1956; reprint ed. Westport, Conn., 1973.